Walker's Guide to
Coigach
& Assynt

Dougie Cunningham

on behalf of the
Coigach & Assynt Living Landscape

Walker's Guide to Coigach & Assynt

Published in the United Kingdom in 2021 by North West Highlands Geopark.

For distribution, contact the North West Highlands Geopark:
admin@nwhgeopark.com

ISBN: 9781914408489
A catalogue record of this book is stored at the British Library.

Front Cover: Stac Pollaidh and Suilven from the Dùbrach Choire Round.
Rear Cover: Suilven and Cam Loch from near Ledmore.

Produced with the support of

This publication has been produced by the
Coigach & Assynt Living Landscape Partnership,
thanks to funding from the National Lottery
Hertiage Fund, and support from the Scottish
Wildlife Trust, Visit Coigach and Discover Assynt.

Contents

Ardvreck Castle, on Loch Assynt.

Overview Map

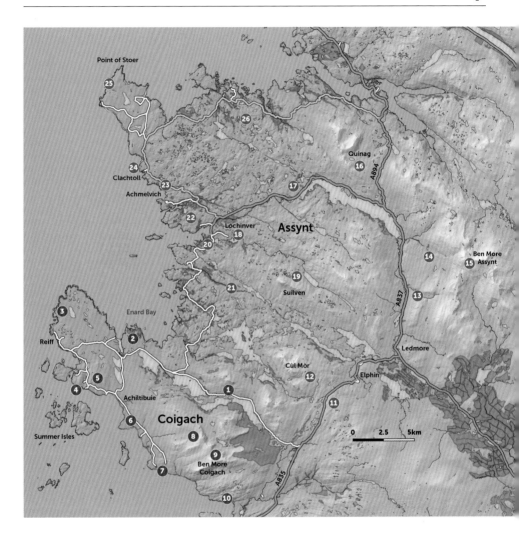

Symbols Used in Route Maps

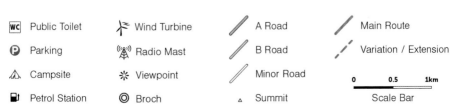

Symbol		Symbol		Symbol		Symbol	
WC	Public Toilet	🗲	Wind Turbine		A Road		Main Route
P	Parking	📡	Radio Mast		B Road		Variation / Extension
⚠	Campsite	❋	Viewpoint		Minor Road		Scale Bar
🔋	Petrol Station	◎	Broch	△	Summit		

Acknowledgements

A huge number of people have pulled together to help produce this guidebook. More work daily to maintain and care for the routes and the environments described in its pages. They all know who they are, but it bears taking a moment to express our gratitude to a few people and groups that have been particularly generous in sharing their knowledge and time throughout the project.

In no particular order, thanks to:

Dr Laura Hamlet

Boyd Alexander

Peter Drake

Assynt Foundation

Badntarbet Estate

Iain Muir

John Muir Trust

NatureScot

Assynt Mountain Rescue Team

Tim Hamlet

Abigail Anne Campbell

Sue Agnew

Culag Community Woodland Trust

The Highland Council Access Officers

Bill Baxter

Seoras Burnett

Visit Coigach Committee

Assynt Development Trust Trustees

Amy Walkingshaw

Chris Puddephatt

Julie Broadfoot

Ray Gibbs

Abi Lightbody

Barry Reid

Sir Chris Bonington

Pete Harrison

Lizzie Williams

Malcolm Bangor-Jones

Don Williams

Mick Ryan

Andy Summers

Ewen McLachlan

Ann Marie Firth-Bernard

Danny Thomson

A list of contributing photographers, along with links to their websites, is on page 127.

Foreword

Every mountain range has its own identity... a flavour that is individual to the area, and which makes it special. Nowhere is this more true than among the Island Mountains of Coigach and Assynt. Gone are the glens that we normally associate with the Scottish Highlands, replaced with vast open plains under huge skies, punctuated by mountains that stand sentinel above the surrounding landscape. Each has its own unique character, and all are instantly recognisable.

Of course, being on the West Coast, there is also boundless coastal walking to be enjoyed. Whether you prefer the beautiful cliffs of Reiff or the perfect sands of Achmelvich, there is something suitable for everyone, and something to discover that you will remember long after you leave.

There is a magic that happens here that makes visitors feel at peace almost instantly. The place itself is an invitation to slow down and engage with nature and our environment. There is more to Coigach and Assynt than just the landscape, however. As with any beautiful place, there is always a community that calls it home.

This guidebook is rooted in that community. It has been a collaborative project, involving local organisations and including contributions from local residents. This book is their invitation to discover their home for yourself, in the hope that you come to love, respect and appreciate it as much as they do themselves.

Sir Chris Bonington CVO CBE DL

Suilven at Sunset.

Introduction

Welcome!

Welcome to Coigach and Assynt. We are the Coigach & Assynt Living Landscape, and while we may be a little biased, we can be pretty confident in saying that this is one of the most beautiful areas in the country, and a walker's paradise.

The landscape here is unique. Island Mountains of beautifully weathered Torridonian Sandstone stand proudly over the cnocs and lochans of the lower Lewisian Gneiss. The geology here is world famous and forms part of the UNESCO endorsed North West Highlands Geopark.

Countless lochs, lochans, rivers and burns collude to make this a place defined as much by water as by rock. Looking out over them from a high vantage, their myriad reflections can make it seem like the land is nothing more than a patchwork of heather and stone, held up against the sky.

Eventually all this water finishes its journey at the coast, where you will find not only some of the most beautiful beaches in the world but also spectacular sea cliffs and, of course, the machair. This fragile, delicate and utterly beautiful habitat is found around the north-west and islands of Scotland, and can be a riot of colour when it blooms in the summer.

At first sight, the landscape of Coigach and Assynt may appear completely remote, however there is an excellent network of paths throughout the area, allowing you to explore at your leisure. This guidebook describes 26 walking routes, ranging in style and character as well as difficulty. Between them they will give you an insight into all the different facets that combine to make this such a special place.

Parking information and detailed directions are provided for each route. Descriptions of how easy or committing a route can be are also provided, to allow you to select something appropriate to your own abilities. We firmly believe that a good walk does not need to be arduous to be deeply satisfying - this is truly the perfect place to simply take some time out, slow down and enjoy the opportunity to reconnect with nature.

Also included is a list of campsites, cafes, public toilets and other facilities, which we hope you find useful during your visit.

As a partnership of local landowners, community interest groups and charities, CALL is investing significant time and resources into local infrastructure, progressive land management, and the safeguarding and promotion of our local heritage. This book is just one project among many towards those ends, and we hope you find that it helps you discover and nurture a connection with the area for yourself.

Coigach and Assynt is a wild, beautiful and working landscape. First and foremost, it is our home. We welcome you to it!

coigach-assynt.org

Getting Around

Driving

Coigach and Assynt are located in the north-west of Scotland, and are relatively sparsely populated. There is a good bus service from Inverness to Ullapool, then a very limited bus service between Ullapool, Lochinver and Drumbeg, which runs once a day. By far the most practical way to get to and around is by car. This alone might be adventure enough for some people!

The main route between Ullapool and Lochinver is a good, two-lane road. Most roads in Coigach and Assynt, however, are small single-track roads with passing places. Drivers new to this style of driving can sometimes find these intimidating.

Thankfully, it's not rocket science, and a few simple rules will make things much easier!

With a little cooperation it all works better than you'd think, and you'll notice that most people give a friendly wee wave to say thanks as they go!

It's worth pointing out that the coastal road between Badnagyle and Lochinver is very windy, and has only tiny passing places - attempts to take larger vans or motorhomes along this road normally end poorly.

6 Secrets to Single-Track Roads

• Take it easy. Blind corners and summits often hide oncoming traffic, and it can be impossible to swerve if you meet someone while going too fast.

• Look ahead. If you see someone approaching, choose a passing place in advance and pull in to allow them to pass.

• Passing places are not parking places!

• When using passing places, always pull up on the left hand side of the tarmac, even if the passing place is on the right hand side of the road.

• Check your mirrors often. If there is even one car behind you for more than a hundred metres, then pull into the next passing place to **allow them to overtake you.**

• Passing places are not parking places - we said that already, but forgetting this can cause real problems, as it essentially blocks the road. Pulling onto the grass at the end of a passing place damages the roadside.

Parking

We've described the best parking areas for each walk throughout the book, and listed coordinates for your sat-nav. We have not included postcodes for the sat-nav, because around here a single code can cover dozens of miles!

As you drive around Coigach and Assynt, there will almost certainly be times when you desperately want to pull in and enjoy the view. There are plenty of places to do this, but please remember that passing places are essential to keeping the roads open - avoid the temptation to park in them, even briefly.

Petrol Stations

We have plenty of hills, water, heather and (in the summer) midges, but petrol stations are few and far-between! It also pays to remember that it can take a lot more fuel to cover a given distance on steep, windy single-track roads as it would on the motorway. Be sure to plan ahead.

There are two fuel stops in the Coigach and Assynt area. The first is in Lochinver, directly across from the Spar store. The second is by the shop in Achiltibuie.

To the south, there's the Lochbroom Filling Station on the main road out of Ullapool towards Inverness.

To the north, there is a small petrol station near the hotel in Scourie.

For those forward-thinking enough to have electric vehicles, at the time of writing there are a couple of charging points in Ullapool, Lochinver and by the Port a Bhaigh campsite.

The hope is that these will quickly become more common, so check zap-map.com or chargeplacesscotland.org for up-to-date information.

Where to Stay

There are countless bed and breakfast or self-catering places to stay in and around Coigach and Assynt, and a handful of hotels. They each offer an ideal base for exploring the area, and a comfortable place to recover after a long day in the hills. The options are too numerous, and change too quickly, to list here. There are other options for people travelling on a more modest budget, and we have outlined them here.

Campsites

There are three campsites in the Coigach and Assynt area. It's worth booking ahead, particularly in the summer season and school holidays.

Port a Bhaigh campsite is in Altandhu, between Reiff and Achiltibuie on the Coigach peninsula. The site is open all year and has space for 50 tents and 42 hard stands. The facilities are as good as the view (which is exceptional!), with a toilet and shower block, and even a licensed grocery store. http://www.portabhaigh.co.uk

There are two sites at Achmelvich. Hillhead Caravans offer stays in their static caravans. Shore Caravan site has static caravans on offer too, as well as space for tents and hook-ups for campervans and caravans. There is a shower block with washing facilities, an on-site shop and even a chip shop through the summer! achmelvich-holidays.co.uk http://shorecaravansite.yolasite.com/

Clachtoll Beach Campsite is just a few miles along the coast from Achmelvich. The beach here is less sheltered but just as beautiful and features views over the famous Split Rock, which appears in the Assynt Crofters' Trust logo. Serviced and un-serviced pitches for tents and vans are available, and the site has good facilities. Flossie's shop is next door to the site, and in summer there is a food van. Clachtoll beach campsite is open all year. https://www.clachtollbeachcampsite.com

Wild Camping

Traditionally, "Wild Camping" meant camping in high or remote spots, far from the road. In recent years, the term is also being used for camping by the roadside but not in a formal campsite. This has led to significant problems in some places, where there can be a small village of tents and campervans assembled almost every night through the summer months. Litter and toilet waste problems can be a serious issue, and spoil the very landscape that these campers have come to enjoy.

If you're planning on sleeping near your car or in a campervan, we'd encourage you to try and use the campsites. If you choose to camp by the roadside instead, please do so responsibly; avoid spots next to houses, and observe any specific notices restricting overnight stays.

Wherever you choose to camp, we implore you to please respect our home, and leave no trace. Always carry a trowel, to assist in burying your toilet waste, and never toilet within 50m of water, paths or roads.

Hostels

There are two hostels in the Coigach and Assynt area. In Coigach, the Acheninver Hostel is located past Achiltibuie, in a beautifully secluded part of the world. It is perfectly situated to enjoy some beautiful walks and has great facilities. https://acheninverhostel.com

In Assynt, the Achmelvich Beach Youth Hostel is beautifully situated, and very friendly with excellent facilities. https://www.hostellingscotland.org.uk/hostels/achmelvich-beach/

Public Toilets

There is a network of public loos that are free to use around the Highlands of Scotland. These tend to be marked as "PC" on OS maps (for Public Conveniences). Here's a list of where to find those in the Coigach and Assynt area.

• **Achiltibuie:** towards the north end of the village, next to a blue information board and a large agricultural shed. Disabled access provided.

• **Knockan Crag:** there are public toilets at the car park for Knock Crag. See page 58 for a description of the walk starting here.

• **Lochinver:** in a small roughcast building on the main road, about 50m south of the police station, or 50m north of the post office. Disabled access provided.

• **Achmelvich:** the public loos are not on the campsite, whose facilities are for customers only. You'll find the public toilets in the car park at the end of the road. No disabled access.

• **Clachtoll:** again, the campsite facilities are for customers only, but there are additional public conveniences by the beach. Disabled access provided.

• **Drumbeg:** a small white building right next to the car park at the viewpoint. Disabled access provided.

• **Kylesku:** next to the car park by the pier, at the end of the road. No disabled access.

• **Stoer Lighthouse:** a community-run facility in the car park by Stoer lighthouse. Disabled access provided.

In addition to the council-run conveniences, some businesses allow public use of their facilities. These locations will display the Highland Comfort Scheme logo.

Both Achmelvich and Clachtoll campsites offer safe disposal facilities for chemical toilets and grey water. A new disposal point by the Sports Centre in Lochinver has also just been opened. Please remember that public toilets are not suitable disposal points.

Cùl Beag and Loch Buine Mòire

Outdoor Access Code

Coigach and Assynt is the perfect place to stop and let yourself breathe.

There are few things better in life than a good walk and taking the time to slow down and just... be. It's like a huge reset button for your mind, and an hour spent watching the clouds skim the mountaintops or an otter play at the waterline does more to relieve tension than a whole weekend binge-watching Netflix.

You don't have to look far to find a place that invites relaxation around here. While there are plenty of beautiful spots that are essentially by the roadside, with just a little thought and preparation you can open up the whole landscape for exploration, adding another level of satisfaction to your experience.

In this book we've described some of our own favourite places, and in doing so we've deliberately tried to include as much variety as possible. This isn't just to showcase the beauty of the area, we hope that it also allows you to find somewhere that speaks to you personally.

Each route has access information provided, to tell you how difficult or committing it will be. This will let you select a walk that is within your ability, and avoid turning what should be a great day out into a bit of an epic. There are a few things to keep in mind regardless of where you go.

Scottish Outdoor Access Code

We're very lucky in Scotland to have a particularly forward-thinking approach to access. With a few common-sense exceptions (like people's gardens), you have the right to responsible access on most land. The word "responsible" is at the heart of the Scottish Outdoor Access Code, and you lose your right of access if you act irresponsibly.

The Code is based on three principles:

- **Respect the interests of other people.** Be considerate of people around you, whether they are the landowners or other visitors to the area. You should also respect other people's property, crops and livestock. If there are sheep or cattle around (or if you're not completely sure that there are none), then dogs should be kept on a lead, regardless of how obedient they normally are.

- **Care for the environment.** There should be no sign of your presence after leaving a place - you should do no damage and leave no litter. You should also not remove anything, even small rocks as a little souvenir - we are lucky to have many thousands of visitors every year and little things very quickly add up.

- **Take responsibility for your own actions.** You are responsible for your own safety and those around you. Some paths are maintained and managed, but you will rarely find fences or warning signs at cliff edges or other hazards. Be mindful of your surroundings.

It is worth specifically pointing out that wood should never be cut for fires. Only 2.5% of Scotland's ancient woodland remains, and taking enough for even a small fire to make a camp special causes damage that takes years to repair. Wood from living trees makes for very poor firewood anyway! Open fires can be beautiful, but pose a very real risk of getting out of hand, and can devastate large areas if they do. Even if contained, they damage the ground upon which they were set. Please think twice.

A more complete list of rights and responsibilities can be found at www.outdooraccess-scotland.com.

Dogs

We love dogs as much as you do, and we want you and your companion to get as much as possible out of your stay. Most dogs that visit the area are not used to being around sheep and other livestock, and even if they're just having fun they can cause the animals a lot of distress.

Every year, perfectly good dogs that are just being playful have resulted in lambs miscarrying and sheep dying, among other things. This is a huge problem for local residents, and will also completely ruin your own day.

If there is any sign at all that there may be livestock in the area, please keep your dogs on the lead - at the very least, it's less of a worry for local crofters and farmers who have seen too many needless losses recently.

There is also a recent trend for people to pick up after their pet and leave the little bag tied to a fence, or tucked into a wall; please don't do this!

Safety

Sometimes accidents happen. With a little forethought and some very basic preparation you can limit the chances of it happening to you, and make sure that if something does then you're ready for it.

Before trying any of the routes in the book, be sure to read the section on Access, which details how difficult it will be. Be realistic about your abilities, and if you're not sure about a particular route then consider trying another instead - we've made sure that there's something in this book for everyone.

Once you're out on a walk, you should never be afraid to turn back, whether that's because you're finding it more difficult than you expected or because the conditions have deteriorated. Every serious walker has retreated from a route at some point, and being willing to do so is one of the simplest ways of keeping yourself safe in the hills.

Cliff edges, riverbanks and other hazards are not signposted or fenced, and it is your responsibility to be aware of your surroundings at all times.

It should be obvious that going out with company is safer than venturing out alone, which can be very committing. Bear in mind that mobile reception can be unreliable. It is good practice to let someone know your plans before you leave, along with what time you expect to return and when they should consider alerting the authorities if you fail to make contact.

In Case of Emergency

If the worst happens and you are unable to walk yourself back to safety, the Mountain Rescue service is there as a last resort. In Scotland, they can be contacted by phoning 999 or 112. When asked, first request the Police then the Mountain Rescue. Be ready with the following information:

• Your location, including a grid reference if possible, and any features that can help describe exactly where you are.

• Information describing the nature of the incident, including the names and ages of any casualties, and the details of any injuries.

Opposite Page: Stac Pollaidh.
Photo: Tim Hamlet

Mountain Rescue training on Quinag.

Equipment

Clothing

The only reliable thing about the Scottish weather is that it's not very reliable. Conditions change quickly, so it makes sense to carry a spare insulation layer and some waterproofs. This should be considered essential on longer walks.

Good footwear makes all the difference. The route described at "Little Assynt Estate" is wheelchair friendly, but all other routes will include uneven, slippy, rocky and boggy ground to at least some extent. Some people prefer a good pair of walking shoes, but if you're not sure then a decent pair of boots is an excellent investment in both comfort and safety.

Safety

A first aid kit should be carried on longer walks, and it's always handy if someone in your group knows how to use it. For larger groups, carrying an emergency shelter is good practice, and every individual should carry an emergency whistle somewhere that is easily accessed. They are cheap, weigh nothing and may save your life. The standard distress signal is six short blasts on the whistle with a pause of a minute before the next six blasts.

This same pattern can be used with a headtorch if it is dark, giving six flashes at a time. This far north, the days can be short through the winter months in particular, and a headtorch should be carried regardless of your intended return time. Be sure to check the batteries before setting off.

Navigation

Some walks described have waymarkers along the route, but not many. This means that you'll need to keep track of where you are and where you are going. For shorter walks, the route descriptions may be sufficient, but for more remote or higher outings a good map and the ability to read it is essential.

We've provided maps of each route in the book, but these are illustrative only and you should carry a printed map and compass for navigation purposes. There are a few options:

• OS Landranger no 15 - Loch Assynt - covers the full Coigach and Assynt area at 1:50k scale.

• OS Explorer no 442 - Assynt & Lochinver - covers the Assynt area at 1:25k scale.

• OS Explorer no 439 - Coigach & Summer Isles - covers the Coigach area at 1:25k scale.

• Harvey BMC - Assynt & Coigach - a superb map that covers the full area at 1:40k scale, with enlargements of Stac Pollaidh, Suilven and Quinag at 1:15k on the reverse.

GPS devices can be useful in certain situations, but are no substitute for a paper map. You should definitely not rely on your phone to navigate. Phone batteries can let you down quickly in cold weather, and the lack of reliable reception means that any maps not permanently downloaded to your device are unlikely to work.

Weather

We have a lot of weather in Coigach and Assynt!

Things can change surprisingly quickly, and when conditions get bad the wind can be fierce. Visibility can quickly drop, and when it does navigation can be difficult. It makes sense to check the weather forecast before heading out, particularly for longer or higher routes. Even a small gain in elevation can expose you to significantly more powerful winds than you might find at the car park.

There are several excellent websites and apps for the weather. A few we particularly like:

• Mountain Weather Information Service - www.mwis.org.uk - a daily forecast specifically tailored towards outdoor activities. The Coigach and Assynt area is covered under the Northwest Highlands forecast.

• Met Office - metoffice.gov.uk - the official UK forecast site, with plenty of information and a dedicated app available.

• WeatherPro - an app available on Android and Apple devices.

Winter walking can bring a fresh set of challenges even to a familiar route. The days up here get very short, with only 6.5 hours of daylight around the solstice, and it is easy to end up walking in the dark on longer routes. Frozen ground can be treacherous, and higher routes may require axe and crampons, and the skills to use them safely. If there is snow on the hills you will need an awareness of avalanche safety. If in doubt, miss it out.

Midges & Ticks

If there's anything that makes Coigach and Assynt fall just ever so slightly short of perfection, it would be the midges and ticks through the summer months.

Midges are tiny biting flies, so small that it's difficult to see individuals in the air. On a still day they can appear in vast clouds. Some people are more sensitive to them than others, and while harmless their bites can cause an irritating itch. Thankfully, midges are only a problem on unusually still days, as even a mild wind keeps them down. They also only appear between mid-May and September. If you're visiting between these times, it's worth carrying a repellent. Smidge, or other Saltadin-based repellents are excellent, being more effective than DEET-based products, and a lot less harmful to use.

Ticks are arguably less irritating than the midges, but as they can occasionally transmit Lyme Disease they are a bit more sinister. Ticks live in the long grasses and foliage and are active between March and around October.

They can crawl some distance up a leg or arm before attaching themselves to you, and once attached can be tricky to remove. It is best to remove them with a dedicated tick removal tool, which many shops in the area will stock. Simply pulling with fingernails or tweezers can damage the tick, leaving the head in your skin and increasing the odds of getting Lymes.

Smidge repels ticks as well as midges, but the best defence is long sleeves, and trousers rather than shorts. Symptoms of Lyme Disease can be vague, but the early stages can appear like mild flu symptoms, tiredness, muscle weakness and headaches. Some people develop a bullseye rash around the site of the bite - if this is present it's a good indicator that you have Lymes, but it does not present in all cases. The disease is normally easily treated if caught early - just be aware, and if in doubt consult a doctor.

Left: a Common Blue butterfly.
Photo: David Haines.

Above: Suilven, from the south.
Photo: Justine Ritchie.

Below: Cul Beag.
Photo: Justine Ritchie.

① Stac Pollaidh

Viewed from afar, Stac Pollaidh seems quite impassable. Tapering to a near vertical wall topped by intricate crenellations and spires, the summit ridge looks like the ramparts of a medieval fortress ready to repel the advances of its larger neighbours, besieging it on all sides.

As unlikely as it looks, there is a good path that will allow you to explore this wonderful wee mountain with relative ease. Only those comfortable with some difficult and exposed scrambling will reach the true summit, but a visit to the more accessible bealach makes for an outing you'll never forget.

Each of the area's Island Mountains has its own unique character. Stac Pollaidh looks by turns intimidating, imposing and inspiring from a distance. Once you are up among the beautifully intricate sandstone sculptures of the ridge it becomes almost playful. Countless nooks and crannies filled with outlandish features are waiting to be discovered afresh on every visit.

Beautifully weathered Torridonian Sandstone features along Stac Pollaidh's summit ridge.

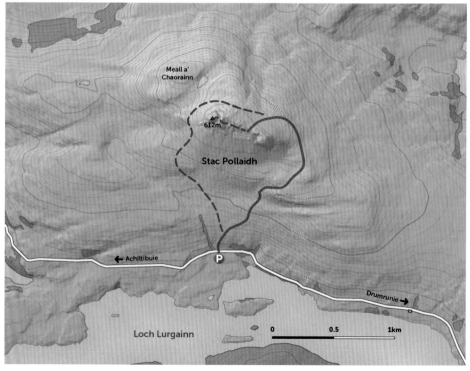

The Route

The path starts directly opposite the car park, and is quite steep from the outset. Once through the trees you'll go through a gate and should follow the right hand fork where the path splits. The gradient eases slightly and the view is good enough to justify plenty of rest stops if needed!

As you track east around the side of the hill you'll enter steeper ground again while the view slowly opens up to the north, with Cùl Mòr and Suilven coming into sight. On the northeast side of the hill the path splits, with the obvious steep route taking you directly to the bealach, or low point, on the ridge. If you've had enough uphill already you can continue northwest on the lower path to complete a circuit around the mountain.

Most people stop at the bealach, where you can enjoy an incredible panorama in every direction, and there is plenty to enjoy without tackling the more difficult sections of the summit ridge.

The red Torridonian Sandstone along the ridge has weathered into all sorts of beautiful and photogenic forms, ready to be discovered with a little exploration by the adventurous. There are many exposed drops, so stay mindful of your surroundings.

The true summit lies at the far western end of the ridge, and reaching it involves a short but difficult scramble above an exposed drop. The view is no better for the extra couple of feet you gain. If you are determined to tick that summit box, please remember it's more difficult to descend the difficult step on your return than than it is to climb on the way out.

To return, descend north off the bealach from the same point you arrived, then retrace the route you climbed. Alternatively, after the initial descent you can head west to traverse around the mountain for a circular route.

Looking back along the summit ridge, with Cùl Mòr and Cùl Beag in the distance.

Access

5km with 550m ascent out and back to the bealach.

6km with 625m ascent out and back to the summit.

The main path from the car park to the bealach is steep but well maintained, and laid with rock to prevent erosion. This makes for uneven walking, so good boots are recommended. Once on the ridge, how far you venture will depend on how comfortable you are with the exposure that some positions can involve. There are many dead ends and false paths, so be mindful of your route back at all times. Always remember that you should never climb up anything you can't climb down!

If completing the circular route on your return, please return to the bottom of the initial descent before turning west, to help mitigate bad erosion further up the hill. This circuit is muddier and more slippy than the outward leg.

Map and compass are recommended.

Parking

Grid Ref: NC 108 096
Lat/Long: 58.035080, -5.2063114

From the main A835 road between Ullapool and Lochinver, take the junction at Drumrunie signposted for Achiltibuie. Stac Pollaidh will be clear ahead of you as you approach on the single-track road. The parking area is directly below the hill and obvious on the southern side of the road. This is a popular route, and despite being a good size, it can be full on busy days. If that's the case then come back later, as parking in passing places essentially blocks the road.

There is a Rock Route interpretation board in the car park, which will give you an insight into the geology you'll see on the walk.

Looking to Cùl Mòr from Stac Pollaidh.
Photo: Dave McBain.

Stac Pollaidh from Loch Lurgainn.

② Enard Bay

Enard Bay in its entirety stretches between the tip of the Rubha Mòr Peninsula of Coigach and Rubha na Brèige by Inverkirkaig in Assynt; to walk the full coast would be quite a mission! Thankfully, this route gives you a great taste of the area and makes the most of the views in a lovely half-day walk that feels more remote than it really is.

The walk starts along the shores of Achnahaird Bay, with great views across the sand flats and dunes. The stretch along the Camas a' Bhothain feels like an adventure on a remote island, and the return south along the top of the shallow cliffs of Creag a' Choin Bhòir enjoys spectacular views across to the iconic Island Mountains of Assynt.

Pack yourself some lunch, and be sure to take your camera or sketchbook - this is a perfect route to slow down, take a deep breath and soak in the ambience.

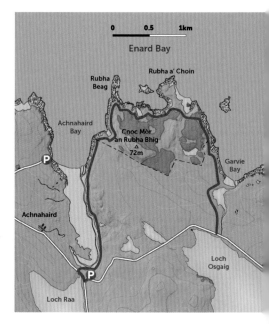

The rocks of Rubha Beag, with the Stoer Peninsula on the distant horizon.

Walking along Achnahaird Bay.

The Route

From the parking area, turn right at the T junction, signposted towards Achnahaird and Reiff. The path starts through a small gate on the right, 50m down the road, just before the bridge over the river. Follow the line of the fence around the southern end of the saltings, before following the riverbank north.

After about 1.5km the flat ground you've been following comes to an end and a short, steep step gains you the heather-clad ground above the rocks that now form the shoreline. The path here is well defined and leads you to a stile over a deer fence.

Once over the fence, the path continues north with beautiful sandstone layers sloping down to the water below, and great views across the Rubha Mòr peninsula to the west. The rocks are perhaps at their most picturesque as you arrive at Rubha Beag, where they rise into jagged ridges as they stretch out into Enard Bay.

Rounding the corner here, you briefly have a great view of the mountains in Assynt before the path drops to the shore. The remains of an old salmon bothy make for a great spot to stop for lunch, with the enclosed bay providing shelter on even the most blustery of days. The path east along Camas a' Bhothain is less defined than previously, but generally if you follow the line of least resistance you won't go too far wrong.

Route finding becomes slightly trickier as you approach the low rocks of Rubha a'Choin at the north eastern end of the peninsula. Turning inland briefly allows you to avoid a short but steep descent, and a short boggy section will take you to the top of Creag a' Choin Mhòir and the clifftop walk back south. From here, the path is once again easy to follow as it leads you to Garvie Bay.

Pass west of the small loch behind the bay, following the path slightly upstream to find the easy crossing points on a couple of burns. The final section to the road is often quite muddy. When you reach the road, turn right and you are just 2km of easy walking from your start-point.

Looking back to Rubha a' Choin from Creag a' Choin Mhoir.

Taking some time to enjoy the ambience at the old Salmon Bothy.

Rubha Beag: Little Headland
Rubha a' Choin: Headdland of Dogs
Camas a' Bhothain: Bay of the Cottage
Creag a' Choin Mhòir: Cliff of the Big Dogs

Parking

Grid Ref: NC 021 124
Lat/Long: 58.056568 , -5.3555549

Taking the road west towards Achiltibuie from the A835, you will reach a T junction next to Achnahaird. Immediately before the junction is a large lay-by parking area, with a red postbox and an information board.

Access

10km circular route.

The terrain is mixed, though things are generally fairly good underfoot. Route-finding can be slightly tricky in a couple of places. There is normally livestock to the south of the deer fence. Part of the reason for the fence is to provide a refuge for wildlife on the peninsula itself, so with that in mind, dogs should be kept on a lead along the whole route.

Loch Garvie and the stream you follow back to the road are both used for fishing. Please give any fishermen a wide berth and avoid disturbing the waters. The boulder dam at the base of the loch is very fragile, so best enjoyed from a distance. If you are interested in fishing here, tickets are available from Mrs Rex at Badentarbat Lodge in Achiltibuie, or in the Achiltibuie Stores.

Rock pools on the approach to Garvie Bay.

A walk to Rubha na Còigeach holds many attractions. Those with an interest in geology will enjoy the cliffs and the sandstone slabs near the northern end of the route. If local history and culture hold more personal appeal, then there are two cleared townships along the way, and more besides.

And if you just like a nice walk in beautiful scenery, then you'll not find much better than this!

The views are varied and the walking constantly interesting. Sea cliffs make for a dramatic start to the route, with more waiting at the farthest point, making Rubha na Còigeach a destination worthy of the distance.

On a still day, this feels like a genuinely idyllic place to be. When the wind is up and there's a good swell from the Minch to launch the waves up the cliffs, it feels wild and exhilarating.

There's every possibility that you came to Coigach and Assynt for the mountains and the sandy beaches, but don't be surprised if this is one of the first walks you tell people about when you get home.

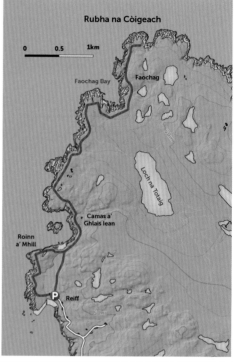

Waves breaking at the base of the cliffs near Roinn a' Mhill.

A good swell before sunset in January.

Access

12km out and back to Rubha na Còigeach.

This route passes through land that is grazed, and all dogs should be kept on a lead. The path is generally quite good, though does fade out from time to time, leaving you to pick your own way along the coast.

Many of the most beautiful features are along the clifftops at the start and end of the walk. Care should be taken near exposed edges, particularly in strong winds or wet weather.

Parking

Grid Ref: NB 965 144
Lat/Long: 58.072215 , -5.4530785

Reiff lies at the very end of the road, at the north-western end of the Rubha Mòr peninsula. Arriving from the Achnahaird direction, the road passes a great viewpoint over the Summer Isles before dropping to a T junction, where you should turn right for Reiff.

Parking is very limited here, with space for a few cars in a layby just before a small bridge over the outflow from the Loch of Reiff. Access is required to the bridge by the croft at all times, and care should be taken not to block the road or the turning space.

The Route

Crossing the bridge over the outflow from the Loch of Reiff will take you to what is known locally as the "Island". It may be a bit of a misnomer, but with so many beautiful features to explore and enjoy, we'll not hold that against it!

On the Island, keen eyes will spot traces of old lazy beds, albeit a lot less distinct here than those seen along the walk to Fox Point or at Clachtoll. Most of the small cairns here are what's known as Clearance Cairns, the result of removing the rocks from the land to make it better for growing crops. There are also the remains of old Kelp Kilns, visible as rock-lined trenches. These are where kelp was burned to create an alkaline ash, used to bleach linens and manufacture soap and glass.

As fascinating as these glimpses into the past are, it is the cliffs along the northwestern part of the Island that are the first highlight of this walk. Be sure to keep an eye out for a large chasm, where the roof of a sea cave has collapsed, leaving a deep slot near Roinn a' Mhill.

If a short walk is all you are looking for, and all the features and scenery of the Island have satisfied you already, you can return directly down the eastern bank of the loch. Turn right when you reach the road to return to the car.

For those wanting a longer outing, the path hugs the coast north around the bay of Camas Eilean Ghlais. Scattered around the bothy at Camas a' Ghlais' lean are the remains of several old houses and buildings.

As you continue north the path eventually peters out, leaving you to find your own route to Rubha Coigach. Stay near the shore and you'll not go too far wrong, though for around a kilometre through the peat hags you may be forgiven for thinking you'd had the best of the walk already. Persevere, for as you round Faochag Bay, both the walking and the views improve, with beautiful Torridonian Sandstone slabs breaking up firmer turf.

The remains of a township can be seen at Faochag, nestled between a series of small lochans. From here, you are more or less at the point of Rubha Còigeach. The cliffs have returned along the coastline, making for some spectacular viewpoints and features. These are some of the most beautiful sea cliffs in all of Coigach and Assynt, and you will doubtless want to take your time to explore before returning back the way you came.

Right: Sunset at Rubha Còigeach.

Below: Exploring some of the ruins along the route.

④ Fox Point

An excellent short walk, taking in one of Coigach's most idyllic spots at Fox Point. The harbour at the starting point in Old Dornie is small but active, and there's a good chance the local fishermen will be at work as you set off. The route picks its way along the coast until it reaches Fox Point, where you'll find the remains of a beautiful old bothy and perfect views in every direction. This is a contender for the best picnic venue in Coigach.

From here, you have three options, the first being to return back along the coastal path. A circular route often makes for a better day out but this walk bears reversing, with the change in direction giving you a fresh outlook over the best features of the day.

Second, you can continue on to Polbain, then walk the single-track roads back to Old Dornie. They are quiet and do make for a lovely walk in themselves.

Finally, for the adventurous, you have the option of returning over the top of Meall Dearg - Gaelic for Red Hill. It's harder going than the coastal route, but the extra elevation does give you a great view over Isle Ristol!

The Route

There are two jetties at Old Dornie harbour. As this book goes to press, the path starts immediately after the second, more westerly one, but it is hoped that this might be moved to start nearer the older jetty over the next couple of years.

As things stand, a signpost will point you in the right direction, and a short steep step will gain you the couple of metres onto the heathery plateau above the shoreline.

You will very quickly find yourself looking out over a shallow, rocky bay. Above it you will see lines of ridges in the ground, which are some of the most well-defined lazy beds in the Coigach area. If you look across to the Isle of Ristol, you'll see more on the hillside there. This was an old technique used to cultivate wetter land that was otherwise difficult to grow on - seaweed would have been piled upon the mounds as fertiliser, and the furrows promoted drainage.

At the far side of the lazy beds is a wooden post, one of several which will mark the route as far as Polbain.

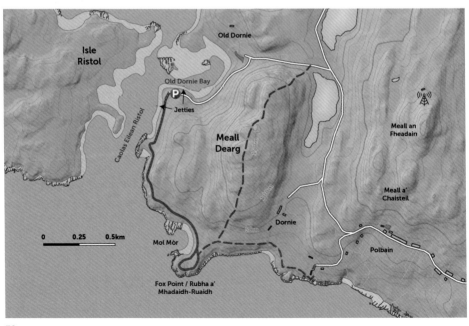

The path sweeps up onto a narrow terrace between the rocky flank of Red Hill inland, and some beautifully featured sandstone cliffs below. The view along this stretch keeps getting better as it opens up to reveal the Summer Isles off the coast, with An Teallach and even the mountains of Torridon to the south.

The terrace ends in a jumble of rocks, and it can be easy to miss the path breaking left, up a rocky ramp to the next terrace above. There is a well-placed marker post at the top of the ramp, easily visible from below should you over-shoot. Take care here - the short, easy scramble can be made more difficult in wet conditions when the rocks can get slippery.

Fox Point is not far ahead now, and it is best to stick close to the shore as you approach. Once there, take plenty of time to explore the rocks and all the vantage points around the remains of an old salmon bothy, used by fishermen operating nearby nets.

Above all else, factor in some time just to sit and enjoy the view. This is a special place.

From here, you must decide on how to return to where you parked. Simply reversing your outward journey makes for an excellent out-and-back walk, but continuing to Polbain and walking back by road is also pleasant.

To do so, follow the path through a series of gates until you reach a minor road by some houses. Follow the road to the junction at the top of the hill and turn left. A kilometre will take you to the turn for Old Dornie harbour, which is another 1.5km down the hill.

For those wanting a bit more of an adventure on the return leg, it is possible to return over the top of Meall Dearg - Red Hill. From the start of the path from Fox Point to Polbain, cut left up the hill. It's steep, and rough walking at times, but the views along the ridge are good. Follow the broad ridge roughly north, then drop northeast down the heathery slopes towards the crossroads between Loch Camas an Fhèidh and Loch a' Mheallain to avoid the crags on the western side of the hill.

The old bothy at Fox Point

Fox Point

Looking towards Ben More Coigach from Fox Point.

Access

3km out and back to Fox Point.
4.5km circular walk returning over Meall Dearg.
5km circular walk, returning by road.

The coastal stretch between Old Dornie and Fox Point is on a good path. If conditions are bad, care should be taken on the one tricky step to gain the second terrace but the route should pose little difficulty to walkers. If returning via the road route, be aware that you will pass through a couple of crofts that often have sheep in the fields, and that dogs should be kept on a leash.

The return over the Meall Dearg is more difficult, with a steep ascent and rough terrain underfoot. Some route-finding skills will be required.

Parking

Grid Ref: NB 983 111
Lat/Long: 58.043255 , -5.4193968

From Achiltibuie, head northwest along the coastal road signposted for Polbain and Reiff. Continue through Polbain, and the road will sweep north past Loch a' Mheallain - this is the stretch of road that is suggested as an option for the return leg of the walk. At the end of the loch, take the left turn signposted for Old Dornie. The harbour is at the end of the road.

This is still a busy working harbour. Even if it's quiet when you arrive, it can fill up with fishermen's vehicles as the tides change, so please try to park considerately.

Red Deer and Suilven, from the Polbain Peat Road.

Local lore says that when work began to build the Polbain Peat Road in 1914 it was started at the top of the road, working back down the hill towards Polbain. Apparently some people believed that if they started at the bottom it would never be finished!

No longer used for cutting the peat, the Polbain Peat Road is now a great short walk that punches well above its weight. With an excellent track and only a modest gain in height, you are treated to some of the best views across the local mountains that you'll find in Coigach. Continuing beyond the Peat Road to reach Meall a' Chaisteil and Meall an Fheadain involves slightly trickier ground that's a whole lot wetter underfoot, but it's not difficult and your reward is a similarly spectacular outlook across the Summer Isles.

If you're looking for a walk with truly memorable panoramic views, but without the physical demands of some of the higher hill days in this book, then look no further. There are a few different options here, and you can tailor your day to suit yourself.

The Route

From the parking spot opposite the arched shed at the eastern end of Polbain, head east down the hill for around 50m to where a paved driveway branches left off the road. This is the start of the Peat Road. The tarmac gives way to a grassy track just after the house about 30m after the junction.

The start of the walk has beautiful views towards Stac Pollaidh and its friends to the east, and Suilven and Quinag will creep into view as the track sweeps around to the north. As you approach the high-point of the Peat Road, a path breaks off to the left, signalled by the first in a line of marker posts. From here, you leave behind the easy, flat track of the Peat Road and start along a wet path through the peat and heather. The path is often vague, but well-spaced marker posts will show you the way if in doubt.

As you start, you look out over the flat peat land between Loch na Creige Duibhe and Lochan Dubh, and can easily see the terraces and lines that are the result of the peats being cut over the years.

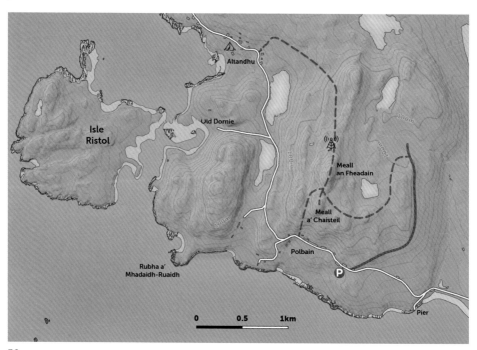

Cùl Mòr, Stac Pollaidh and Cùl Beag from the bealach between Meall Chaisteil and Meall an Fheadain.

The marker posts will lead you around the south of Lochan Dubh towards the bealach between Meall a' Chaisteil and Meall an Fheadain. There's a natural attraction to the high point of any area, but you'd do well to visit the top of Meall a' Chaisteil before going up its slightly higher neighbour. This small summit offers an unrivalled view over the Summer Isles and is one of the finest viewpoints in the area.

Crossing back over the saddle and climbing Meall an Fheadain will take very little time, and once there it is easy to see why it was used as a lookout point to observe shipping in the Minch during WW2. From here, you have three options. Arguably the most satisfying is to reverse your route, returning back to Badentarbat Beach the way you came, enjoying the fresh take on the views this allows.

If you would like a shorter circular route, then return to the low point between the two summits, then follow the marker posts west and then south-west down the hill. They will take you down a decent path to rejoin the road just west of Polbain, leaving you with an easy kilometre walk along the road to finish.

Alternatively, continue north over the top of Meall an Fheadain to meet the access track that services the masts. Following this for two kilometres will bring you out near the campsite (and the pub!) in Altandhu - a perfect choice if you have someone there to collect you! If not, then the walk back to your starting point along the road is more enjoyable than you might expect.

Meall an Fheadain: Hill of the Chanter
Lochan Dubh: the Dark Lochan
Meall a' Chaisteil: Castle Hill
Loch na Creige Duibhe: Loch of the Black Rock

37

Above: The Summer Isles, from Meall a' Chaisteil.

Right: The grassy track at the start of the Polbain Peat Road.

Parking

Grid Ref: NC 003 099
Lat/Long: 58.033126 , -5.3857566

From Achiltibuie, follow the coastal road towards Polbain, turning up the hill above the pier. As the gradient eases, there is an arched boat shed on the right hand side of the road, and space for a couple of cars to park directly across the road. If this spot is full then you can park at the pier in Badentarbat and walk the 700m up the hill to reach the turn onto the Peat Road.

Access

7.5km with 220m ascent as a through route to Altandhu

12km with 220m ascent out and back to Meall an Fheadain.

The Peat Road is an excellent grassy track with only a gentle incline, and makes for very easy walking. If continuing to the top of the hill, you will be crossing open moor and the path can be very vague in places. Well-spaced marker posts will point the way, but you'll appreciate a good pair of waterproof boots!

Achlochan is a trove of local history. On a walk around the peninsula you'll pass the remains of a 2000 year old broch, with the ruins of much more recent croft buildings surrounding it. You'll see the recesses cut into the shore to shelter boats in a bygone era, and the stone-lined depressions that were used as kilns to burn kelp. There is even the machinery from a WWI rifle range.

Ground-nesting birds like the curlew, snipe, oystercatcher and Meadow Pipit nest here. Reed beds - the largest of their type in Wester Ross - which once provided thatch for local houses are now home to Reed Buntings, Sedge Warblers and Corncrakes.

There's plenty to explore along this walk, but it is equally lovely just to sit on the rocks at Rubha Dùnan, and enjoy the tranquility of the view across the water to the distant mountains.

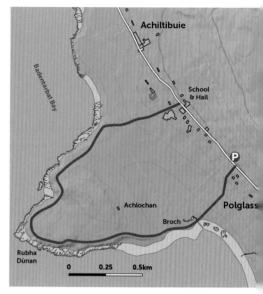

The Route

The route starts just a few metres west along the main road from the parking area, where a wooden signpost will point you towards the broch and coast. The path starts between some houses, before two gates release you into croft land and you have a short walk to the shore. Arriving at the stoney beach, you'll see a Beach Clean Station, where some bin bags and litter pickers are available. Debris constantly washes up along the shore, so should you want to help keep the area clean, your efforts will be greatly appreciated!

As you walk west around the bay you can't help but enjoy the tall reeds growing inland, but also keep your eyes out for the remains of an old boat naust. This was a narrow pit cut into the head of the beach that a boat would have been hauled into for shelter.

There are also kelp kilns here, where kelp was burned to make alkaline ash that was used to bleach linen and manufacture glass and soap. The kelp industry crashed in the 1820s when other means of producing alkali were developed, leading to poverty in areas that relied upon it.

Very quickly you will reach the remains of several old buildings, giving a hint of what life would have been like when the area was more heavily populated and people lived off the land. Looking back towards the road, you'll see a line of abandoned houses standing at the top of their crofts. Between the buildings of the old croft on the shore you will see the circular form of the old iron-age broch around which they were built.

The path continues west out towards the rocky point of Rubha Dùnan. On a calm day this can be a very tranquil place to sit and enjoy the view, and feels wonderfully isolated from the world. Follow the marker posts around the northern side of the peninsula, and eventually back to a gate by the old Rifle Range. This was used to train recruits to the Seaforth Highlanders and the Lovat Scouts. Almost half the men serving in Highland regiments in the First World War never returned home - a disproportionate number compared with other regiments.

From here, it is a short walk on a made path to reach the road, where a right turn and a little over half a kilometre walk will return you to your car.

Above: the view from Rubha Dùnan.

Below: Looking down on the broch and croft ruins.

Parking

Grid Ref: NC 033 073
Lat/Long: 58.011197 , -5.3311833

The Achlochan peninsula is easily spotted as you drive towards Polglass from Achiltibuie. Continue past the Community Hall for almost a kilometre to a rough parking area almost directly opposite the start of the walk, just before a couple of houses.

Access

4km circular walk.

This is a great short walk, on easy terrain throughout. The path is narrow but easy to follow, and there are marker posts along the way to keep you right. Sheep graze the land, and there have been issues in recent years with dogs, so please keep them on a lead. This will also help the birds that nest on the ground here from April to September.

This is an easy circular walk, with some beautiful views. Most of the distance covered is along quiet roads, with 1.5km of the 8km total being on a well-defined path. The loop can be done in either direction, but taking it counter-clockwise as described gives you the best views towards Isle Martin, and giving you a good look along the improbable route of the Postie's Path as it traverses the base of the cliffs to the south-east. It also means that your return leg will take you along the higher road, with the gained height improving the views over the Summer Isles - a great evening wander!

The Route

Once parked, continue along the single track road almost 500m until you reach a fork in the road. Go right, following the road towards Achduart, with Loch Broom below. The mountains of Wester Ross and the Summer Isles work together to ensure that the entire horizon is full of interest. Inland, Ben More Coigach commands the skyline, along with the Acheninver Pinnacle on Cona Mheall.

Culnacraig: Back of the rock
Achduart: Field at the Black Headland
Achnacarnin: Field at the Shoreline (or lip)
Acheninver: Field at the River Mouth
Cona Mheall: Hill of Enchantment

The paved road ends by a small turning circle, where a stone waymarker points the way towards Strathcanaird and Culnacraig. Follow its direction, taking the dirt track along the line of the telegraph poles. A second marker will direct you through a series of gates, passing an information board as you go. A good path will carry you from here, passing a well-placed bench with a great view south, which makes for the perfect spot for a brew if you've brought a flask.

Shortly after the path diverges from the line of the telegraph poles the view south-east along the coast opens up. From here you have a perfect view along the line of the Postie's Path, which snakes along the coast near the bottom of the cliffs in a route every bit as exposed and tricky as it looks from a distance. It is hard to imagine the dedication and fortitude that the postman must have had to walk this route twice a week in the 1860s!

A third stone route marker is found just after a footbridge over a pretty little gorge, directing us up to the left through Culnacraig where the path rejoins the road. The 3km back along the road to your car are straightforward, with no difficulties to distract from the views northwest to the Summer Isles.

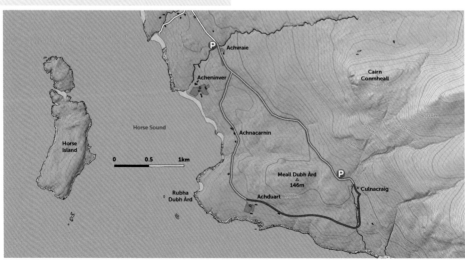

Ben More Coigach disappearing into the clouds above Culnacraig.

Parking

Grid Ref: NC 045 060
Lat/Long: 57.999971 , -5.3101624

From Achiltibuie, drive southeast towards Culnacraig, stopping to park by the roadside in the layby signposted for the Youth Hostel at Achvraie. If you reach the fork in the road signposted for Achduart, you have gone too far.

Access

8km circular walk.

This walk is mostly on quiet, paved roads, with the stretch between Achduart and Culnacraig being a good path. It passes several small townships where there may be livestock roaming freely - please keep dogs on a lead.

Culnacraig

The remains of a bronze age hut circle above the shore suggest that the area around Culnacraig has seen human habitation for over 3000 years, though local records suggest that there was nobody living here in the mid-17th to 18th centuries. People returned when they were forced from more fertile lands elsewhere during the clearances.

On arriving, they lived closer to the sea than the houses at Culnacraig today, probably in hastily-built turf houses. Rumour has it that one family spent the first year in a cave by the sea. In time, the turf houses were replaced with stone, and the marshes drained to be turned into the fertile fields that are still in use.

Looking north to the mountains, from the walk along An t-Sàil on the Dubrach Choire Round.

8 Dùbrach Choire Round

It could be argued that the Dùbrach Choire Round suffers for its proximity to the Ben More Coigach circuit. If not for the fact that it is immediately next door to one of the classic mountain walks in the area, this route would undoubtedly see a lot more traffic and be justifiably famous in its own right.

It may not boast the high point in the range or feature in as many blogs but the walking is superb, varied and interesting, and comes with views that easily rival any you'll find among the Scottish mountains. The icing on the cake is that with the hypnotic draw of Ben More Coigach just along the road, there's every possibility that you'll have the place to yourself.

This is a long and challenging walk, on mixed and often difficult terrain. Experienced walkers will leave feeling like they've discovered a hidden gem.

Stac Pollaidh as seen from Creag Dubh na Sàile.

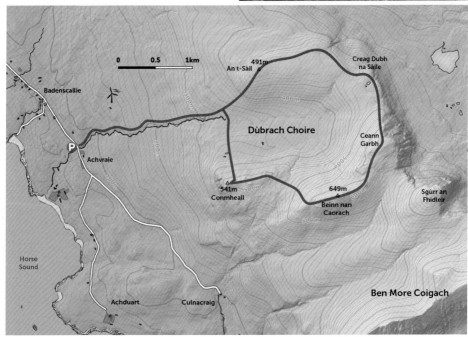

The Fiddler and Ben More Coigach, from Ceann Garbh. Photo: Chris Puddephatt.

The Route

The walk starts directly opposite the Youth Hostel car park at Achvraie, with an ill-defined path that follows the northern bank of the Allt Ach' a' Bràighe. This first part of the route is wet underfoot and, in all fairness, not a great advertisement for the rest of the day. Don't let it put you off! Stay close to the edge of the shallow gorge the burn runs through, and you won't go too far wrong.

Follow the gorge for around 2km past a series of beautiful waterfalls until you reach the obvious concrete water intake on the burn. From here, break left to head directly up the side of An t-Sàil, picking the path of least resistance up the open hillside. This is hard going, and the summit can feel quite elusive as you climb the convex hillside. A cairn marks your arrival on the broad plateau.

It would be tempting to stick to the centre of the plateau as you walk east, but tending towards the northern edge allows for much more expansive views along the Rubha Còigeach peninsula to the north-west and across Loch Bad a' Ghaill towards Stac Pollaidh, Suilven and Quinag to the north-east. When you reach Creag Dhubh na Sàile the uninterrupted view over the Island Mountains is absolutely spectacular.

From Creag Dubh na Sàile follow the ridge south-east, staying as near to the eastern edge as is practical as you navigate the peat hags. A short but steep climb takes you up to another plateau on Ceann Garbh, with great views of the pointed summit of Sgùrr an Fhidleir further south along the ridge, and Beinn an Eòin across the steep little glen of An Clù-nead.

Head south-west from the top of Ceann Garbh, crossing a broad bealach towards Beinn nan Caorach, whose sandstone ridge has weathered into weird, beautiful shapes. As the ridge starts to descend towards the sea, turn right to cross the coll leading to Conmheall. Heading west on the ridge here is some of the most interesting walking of the day, and as the ridge narrows you have unobstructed views spanning the mountains of Torridon, Skye and even Lewis and Harris across the Minch.

From the summit cairn at the very end of the ridge, return 100m back along the way you came before dropping off the ridge to the north on a steep boulder slope. There's no path to speak of, but aim for two small lochans, then continue down to meet the Allt Ach' a' Bràighe where you left it earlier in the day. Return to the car by descending the same route as your approach.

Dùbrach Choire: Dark Corrie
Allt Ach' a' Bràighe: Burn of the Field of the Brae
An t' Sail: The Heel
Loch Bad a' Ghaill: Clumps Loch
Creag Dubh na Sàile: Black Cliff of the Heel
Ceann Garbh: Rugged Head
Beinn nan Caorach: the Hill of the Sheep
Cona Mheall / Conmheall: the Hill of Enchantment

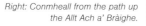

Right: Conmheall from the path up the Allt Ach a' Bràighe.

Parking

Grid Ref: NC 045 060
Lat/Long: 57.999971 , -5.3101624

From Achiltibuie, drive southeast towards Culnacraig, stopping to park by the roadside in the layby signposted for the Youth Hostel at Achvraie. If you reach the fork in the road signposted for Achduart, you have gone too far.

Access

11km with 750m ascent circular route.

This is a long and physical day in the hills. The terrain is mixed and frequently difficult underfoot, often with little to no path to speak of. Good route finding is essential, and walkers will want a map, compass and the skills to use them if considering a day on the Dùbrach Choire round. In poor weather, consider an alternative.

Above: Quinag, Suilven and Stac Pollaidh.

Below: looking over the Summer Isles from the descent at dusk.

When first sighted on the drive north out of Ullapool, Ben More Coigach appears as a vast wall of rock. Three kilometres of unbroken cliffs topped by an almost perfectly flat skyline give the illusion of a squat, bulky mountain. The fact that it is known locally as "the Rock" seems to support this notion, yet there is so much more to Ben More Coigach than first meets the eye.

The formidable south-eastern wall is just one end of a much greater massif which tapers through a succession of coires and ridges towards the Minch. Atop the wall itself is an exceptional ridge walk among intricately weathered pinnacles. If you're lucky it can be enjoyed in the company of some golden eagles.

This horseshoe route begins with an ascent of Sgùrr an Fhìdhleir - a neighbouring summit with one of the best views on the west coast - before continuing around Ben More Coigach itself. Along the way you'll enjoy some of the finest walking in the area, with the opportunity for some easy scrambling and a taste of adventure for those who seek it.

The Route

From the walkers' car park, continue along the road towards Culnacraig, crossing a bridge after around 300m. Just after the bridge, you start the climb towards Sgùrr an Fhìdhleir by heading directly up the hillside. The going is initially quite steep and the path is a little vague at first, but quickly consolidates.

After around a kilometre the gradient eases and the route up the broad ridge towards the Fiddler is straightforward. Beautiful plates of frost-shattered Torridonian Sandstone cover the summit, and in the last few metres of ascent the view vaults out over the mountains to the north. In stark contrast to the gentle slope you have climbed, the land drops near vertically to the north and you suddenly feel yourself to be among the mountains rather than the hills.

Descend south from the Fiddler then track east along the top of the cliffs known as the Black Flags, above Lochan Tuath towards Ben More Coigach. Another steep ascent will take you to the start of the long traverse along the mountain.

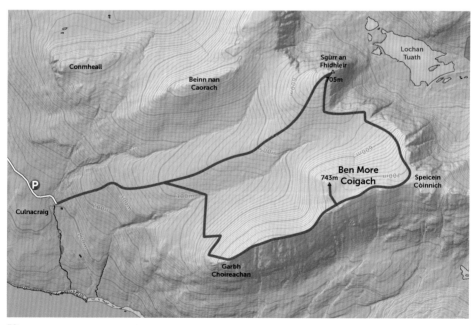

The climb ends on a broad plateau. A brief foray east to the top of Speicein Còinnich - the Mossy Peak - is enjoyable but entirely optional before you head south-west towards the summit and the ridge beyond. It's worth staying towards the southern side of the plateau to enjoy the best of the views, diverting north to reach the obvious summit shelter a kilometre along the ridge.

Continuing south-west from here, the walking gets more involved! In good conditions, sticking to the crest of the ridge makes for some great terrain, with some easy scrambling past beautiful rock features, with just enough exposure to focus the mind. The difficult sections can be bypassed on the north side of the ridge.

Continue over the high point of ridge, towards Garbh Choireachan, and as the descent starts to steepen take the path of least resistance down the slopes north towards Allt nan Coisiche. The path can be difficult to follow here, but aim to cross the burn just before the start of the steep-sided gorge, then walk west until you meet the path where you started your ascent earlier in the day. From here, it is a short descent back to the road.

Beautifully eroded Torridonian Sandstone features on the summit of Sgùrr an Fhìdhleir, above, and on the ridge of Ben More Coigach, below.

Above: Looking along the ridge to Garbh Choireachan.

Right: easy scrambling along the ridge.

Parking

Grid Ref: NC 062 042
Lat/Long: 57.984673, -5.2796432

From Achiltibuie, continue along the road towards Culnacraig. Just before the road makes its final descent to the township, there is a small walkers' car park on the northern side of the road.

Access

11km with 875m ascent circular route.

This mountain day takes in a mixture of terrain. The path is difficult to follow in places, and the going can be hard underfoot. The scrambling along the ridge is generally only as difficult as the route you choose, but there will always be at least a moderate level of exposure. Map, compass and the skills to use them are needed.

This is an exceptional day out that you will remember and relive for a long time. In keeping with the very best walks it has a history and story as impressive as the landscape it passes through. Looking along the coast the route looks completely improbable. Traversing along the steep flanks of Ben More Coigach, it threads its way through complex and difficult ground.

Walking the route is known locally as "Taking the Rock". Indeed, Culnacraig takes its name from the Gaelic, *Cul Na Creighe,* meaning "back of the rock".

Back in the 17th and 18th centuries, church-goers travelled from Achiltibuie to the church at Clachan, at the far end of Loch Broom, by Taking the Rock. The route was also used to transport livestock to market from the townships of Coigach.

Later, in the 1860s, the post office employed Kenneth McLennan to carry the post to the communities of Coigach by the same route. It was a contract that remained in his family for over 50 years.

Taking the Rock today, it is difficult not to marvel at how hardy previous generations must have been to navigate such a path so regularly. Make no mistake; for all that this is a low-level traverse, the walking is hard, route-finding is difficult and several parts of the path are very exposed above considerable drops.

Experienced walkers with a head for heights will love the Postie's Path, but if that doesn't sound like you, consider walking some of the coastal paths between Culnacraig and Achiltibuie instead.

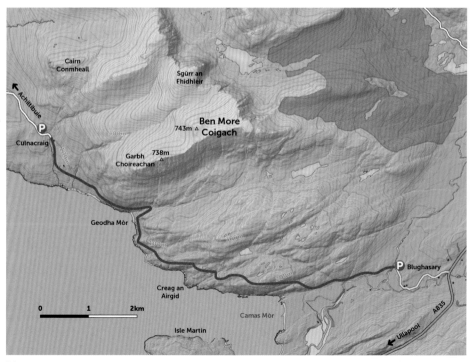

A modern, stone route marker along the Postie's Path.

One of the older, but more frequent wooden posts.

The Route

From the car park at Blughasary, the route starts by crossing the river where the path is clearly signposted to the left after the bridge. The first part of the walk follows the line of a deer fence and is quite straight-forward. After 2km you come to a signpost before a stile over the fence. Take the right-hand fork, signposted for "Achiltibuie 9 1/2 miles", to climb steeply up the hill. The path is deeply eroded in places and often very muddy.

After a short climb the route swings left to start the long traverse to Culnacraig. A mixture of stone route markers and older wooden posts will help keep you on the right route through those areas where the path can be difficult to identify. At times the terrain ahead looks quite improbable, and you must place your trust in the generations that have gone before to have found the least-difficult route through the myriad obstacles. Short scrambles are quickly followed by boggy traverses, and the route-finding is consistently demanding to the point you need to remain aware of your surroundings at all times.

Almost 5km into the walk, where you find yourself looking over Creag an Airgid and Isle Martin to the south, you reach one of the most exposed sections of the day. The path narrows and slinks along the top of some cliffs, with enough exposure to focus the mind of even the most confident walkers.

The mixed terrain continues as the views around you slowly change, until you meet a small gorge just beyond a rocky bay and Geodha Mòr. The path takes an abrupt turn inland here, running along the line of a fence until it reaches a good point to ford the Allt a' Choire Mhòir. On returning to the coast you are straight into yet another airy traverse.

This section marks the last of the difficulties and the slopes on either side quickly ease as you approach Culnacraig. Just below the cottages, the path meets the coastal path to Achduart. Follow the directions towards Culnacraig, and continue up the road to the car park at the top of the hill, where you hopefully have a vehicle waiting, or someone to collect you and hear about your adventures!

Difficult route-finding on exposed terrain.

Parking

This is a through-route, between Blughasary and Culnacraig. It is best to arrange to leave a vehicle at the far end of the walk before starting, or have someone collect you when you finish.

Blughasary
Grid Ref: NC 135 015
Lat/Long: 57.963477 , -5.1544523

7 miles north of Ullapool, at the low point on the A835, take the single track road signposted for Blughasary. There is a small car park at the end of the road. Pay heed to the warning about wider vehicles, as there is a very narrow spot between a building and a large rock.

Culnacraig
Grid Ref: NC 064 042
Lat/Long: 57.984212 , -5.2801087

Follow the minor road through Achiltibuie and continue heading south-east towards Culnacraig. The car park is an obvious gravel area just before the road drops down to Culnacraig.

Access

11km through-route.

This is a long, hard day on rough terrain, with difficult route-finding and several very exposed sections.

The path itself is difficult underfoot and often hard to identify, despite a mixture of old wooden and more recent stone marker posts pointing the way. This can be particularly true in the summer months where heather and bracken can further obscure it. Parts of the path can be very slippery, often above long, unprotected drops where a fall would be fatal.

Map and compass will be required, with both 1:50k and 1:25k OS maps having the route marked. The Postie's Path is recommended only for experienced walkers with a good head for heights.

Creag an Airgid, with Isle Martin behind.

11 Knockan Crag

The paths at Knockan Crag make for a great short walk, with views across to the twin summits of Cùl Mòr, and Stac Pollaidh out to the west. There's much more here than just the views across neighbouring hills, however; within the rocks here you'll see some of the features that have made this an essential destination for geologists for more than 100 years.

The Rock Room is reached by an all-abilities path and has an excellent collection of displays to help you appreciate not just the story of how the hills and mountains before you were formed, but also how geologists pieced together that story from the fragments of evidence all around us. Venturing further, you'll see prime examples of this evidence showcased in path-side displays.

Artists have also put together a series of sculptures related to the story of Knockan Crag, which are spread along the length of the circular walk around the crags.

The Route

There are three signposted routes at Knockan Crag. Each starts from the Rock Room - an open visitor centre with excellent information and exhibits about the surrounding landscape. It's just a short distance along an all-abilities path from the car park. As you start that path you will pass the "Knockan Puzzle", a miniature representation of some of the rocks that make up the crags and a hint at what's to come.

The shortest trail is a circular walk down to the remains of an old quarry, where you will find some Pipe Rock - the fossilised remains of worm burrows, which create beautiful vertical stripes through the pink rock. There is also an inscription of some words from the poet Norman MacCaig - if you grow to love Assynt during your visit you could do worse than to read more of his writing.

The Thrust Trail will take you along the base of the crags to an exposed part of the rock at the boundary of the Moine Thrust. You will be able to clearly see the difference between the dark Moine rocks above and the lighter limestone rocks below. It was the puzzle of how these older rocks came to be sitting on top of the younger limestone that helped the geologists Peach and Horne figure out how rocks moved over deep time.

From the end of the Thrust Trail you can return the way you came, or continue along the path to complete the Crag Top Trail. This circular route loops around the top of the crags, returning you to the car park from the south. A rough set of uneven stairs has been built from local rock to aid the climb up to the top of the crags, and the path is good throughout its length. There are a couple of great viewpoints as well as more installations to enjoy along the way.

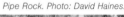

Pipe Rock. Photo: David Haines.

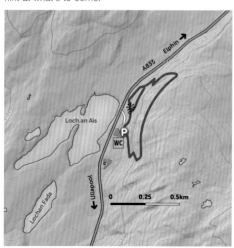

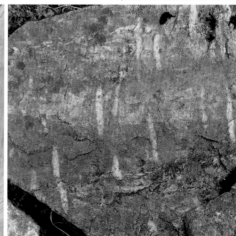

The Knockan Puzzle, at the start of the all-abilities path to the Rock Room.

The Moine Thrust

Just how does a layer of 1000 million year old rock end up sitting on top of rocks that are "only" 500 million years old? This question was at the heart of a huge debate among scientists in the mid to late 1800s. In the process of answering it, the geologists Peach and Horne changed our understanding of how the world works.

When you look at a cross-section of the rocks at Knockan Crag, things start as you would expect, with the ancient Lewisian Gneiss as the bottom layer, dating back three billion years. On top of that is a layer of old Torridonian Sandstone, which is one billion years old, and was deposited by rivers onto a land surface. Then follows a layer of Basal Quartzite, then Pipe Rock, the Fucoid Beds, Salterella Grit and Durness Limestone - sedimentary rocks laid down by the sea between 540 and 500 million years ago, and getting "younger" as you go up through the layers, exactly as you'd expect.

Directly above the pale Durness Limestone is a layer of dark Moine rocks, a different type of rock altogether. These started as sandstones and mudstones but were changed under huge pressure during a mountain building phase. The Moine rocks have been dated to 870 million years ago - hundreds of millions of years older than the layer directly below them at Knockan Crag! All these layers are all beautifully represented in the "Knockan Puzzle" installation at the start of the path to the Rock Room.

After years of research, Peach and Horne figured out how this irregularity - or unconformity - came to be. They called the process "Thrust Faulting", and this particular area was named the "Moine Thrust Zone", after the great A' Mhòine bog by Loch Eriboll.

Rocks aren't as static as they look, they just move very slowly, in deep time. The earth's crust consists of several rigid plates; huge sheets of rock that move around the planet over the course of millions of years. When two plates collide, the rocks where they meet get squeezed together under huge pressures, and sometimes whole slabs of rock get thrust upwards, over the top of the other rocks.

The older, bottom layer of one plate then sits above the youngest layer that was at the top of the other plate!

Above: One of the sculptures along the Crag Top Trail, with a stunning view to Ben More Coigach.

Below: The Thrust Trail at Knockan Crag.

Sculptures of geologists Peach and Horne at the Rock Room.

Parking

Grid Ref: NC 187 090
Lat/Long: 58.033933 , -5.0706524

Knockan Crag has an excellent car park just off the main A835 Ullapool-Ledmore road 2.5 miles south of Elphin, just across the road from Lochan an Àis.

Access

400m for the Quarry Trail.

700m for the Thrust Trail.

2km for the Crag Top Trail.

The path as far as the Rock Room is all-abilities accessible. Beyond there, the trails are narrower but very good. The climb up to the top of the crags is short but steep, and just exposed enough that those who are actively afraid of heights or not confident on uneven ground may find it a bit of an adventure.

The public toilets in the car park are open 24/7.

The view to Stac Pollaidh and beyond, from the summit of Cùl Mòr in winter.

Suilven from the summit of Cùl Mòr.

Cùl Mòr is the highest of the area's Island Mountains, and an ascent is a pretty magnificent way to spend a day. The view as you climb from the east is dominated by Canisp and the Ben More Assynt massif to the north, and An Teallach and the distant mountains of Torridon to the south. Suilven teases you along the way, popping in and out of view like the big mysterious lump of rock that it is.

Not until the final few metres to the summit does the view open up across Coigach to the south, and this is the real prize. From here, Cùl Beag combines with the complex northern flanks of Ben More Coigach and its satellites to provide a show-stopping vista, with the fin of Stac Pollaidh completing the scene to the west. All around you, the lochs and lochans glimmer among the heather.

This is without doubt one of the best mountain days in the area, and any serious walker will love it.

The Route

A good stalker's path starts from the northern end of the roadside car park, and will carry you easily for the first part of the walk. A little under 3km into the walk the made track ends and the path continuing up the hill then spreads and splits. It can be vague in places but a line of small cairns will guide you directly to the small rise of Meallan Diomhain, where you have a beautiful view of the twin summits of Cùl Mòr ahead.

The main summit is the northern one, on the right as you face them, and we will approach essentially along the northern skyline. From the cairn atop Meallan Diomhain head north, skirting the side of a small lochan before trending west, along the top of Cadha nan Each.

The ridge line will lead you around to the south, directly up the steepening slopes to the summit. The final few hundred metres is a boulder field and difficult underfoot, but the view at the top is more than ample reward.

Once you've had time to absorb the views across Cùl Beag, Ben More Coigach and Stac Pollaidh, you will likely notice the stark change in the rocks as you walk away from the summit shelter, from the pale, angular Cambrian Quartzite to the more rounded, deep red Torridonian Sandstone. If time permits, the walk out and back along Sròn Gharbh is worthwhile for an unobscured view across Loch Sionascaig.

The obvious descent is to retrace your steps. Alternatively, you can visit the second summit, Creag nan Calman, to the south before descending east from the bealach between the peaks. A little over a kilometre of rough terrain will return you to the cairn at Meallan Dìomhain where you rejoin your original route for the remainder of the walk back to the car park.

Looking south to Cùl Beag from the summit.

Cambrian Quartzite & Torridonian Sandstone

The bulk of Cùl Mòr is Torridonian Sandstone, which is formed from sediments deposited on land by rivers 1000 million years ago. These rivers flowed from mountains in what is now Greenland and Canada, when that land was much closer, before the Atlantic Ocean opened.

Rock is only stationary from our brief viewpoint, and over the next 400+ million years the Torridonian Sandstone layers were tilted, and then eroded by the sea. Today, these rocks appear deep red or brown in colour, and tend to weather into beautiful curves and round plates.

Around 540 million years ago the area would have been under shallow coastal waters and the Cambrian Quartzite layer was laid down as more sediment on top of the eroded Torridonian. The Cambrian Quartzite is made almost entirely of tiny grains of quartzite crystals and appears as a pale grey or light pink rock, with very straight edges and angular corners.

A later mountain-building era tilted the area eastwards, leaving the originally horizontal Quartzite layers at an angle of around 15 degrees. Much later again, huge glaciers rolled through the area, shaping the mountains as we see them today. These processes are all beautifully explained in the Rock Room at Knockan Crag - see page 58.

Part of the Cambrian Quartzite layer still remains on the eastern side of a few local mountains. Much of the ascent of Cùl Mòr is on this "younger" rock, and both summits are high enough to protrude into this layer. As you walk west from the summit towards Sron Gharbh you effectively walk backwards through millions of years into the older Torridonian layers. You'll see a similar transition as you walk over the summit of Spidean Coinich on Quinag.

Looking west from the end of Sron Gharbh over the cnocs and lochans, you are looking down upon an even older layer of Lewisian Gneiss, which lies beneath the Torridonian Sandstone.

Cùl Mòr

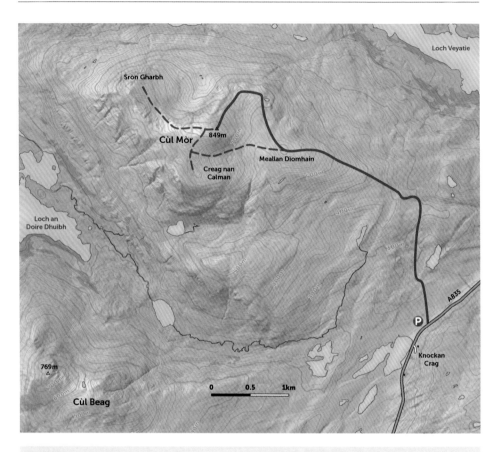

Parking

Grid Ref: NC 189 094
Lat/Long: 58.036665, -5.0691923

Roadside parking is available in a large lay-by immediately north of the well-signposted Knockan Crag car park on the A835, a couple of miles south of Elphin.

Access

14km with 800m ascent for both summits.

This is a long mountain day. Experienced hill walkers will find few difficulties but some route-finding skills are needed and map, compass and the knowledge and skills to use them are essential. Bear in mind that visibility can deteriorate rapidly.

The route starts on a good stalker's path, progressing into a wet tramp up the boggy hillside following a line of cairns. The final ascent is up a boulderfield which is difficult underfoot. Only attempt this route in winter if you have sufficient winter walking experience with axe and crampons.

Above: the steep boulderfield leading to the summit.
Photo: Chris Puddephatt.

Below: Cùl Beag from Cùl Mòr
Photo: Chris Puddephatt.

⑬ Bone Caves

The Bone Caves have fascinated archaeologists and geologists alike since the late 1800s, when their first tentative excavations turned up bone fragments from various animals.

Bones excavated from the caves hint at wildlife that is no longer seen in Scotland, with bear, reindeer, lemming, lynx, wolf and arctic fox remains all being found within this one cave complex, making it the most complete record we have of animals who lived in Scotland in the last glacial period. Some of these date as far back as 47,000 years, which is before the last ice age! Human bones have also been found, dating back around 4,500 years.

The caves themselves started to form over 200,000 years ago, when flowing water shaped tunnels through the soft Durness Limestone. Later, glaciers carved out the glens we see today, and where they met the tunnels they left the caves as openings in the crags. Since then, it would seem that the caves have provided shelter for animals and early humans alike.

It is a relatively short and easy walk to the caves, and as you go up through the secluded glen it is easy to imagine the modern world melt away behind you. You'll pass the springs where the Allt nan Uamh bubbles from the ground, and as you watch the deer on the hillside it is hard not to wonder what else might have been out there alongside them thousands of years ago.

The Route

From the car park, go through the gate and follow the obvious path leading upstream along the northern side of the river. The initial stretch is easy going and passes some nice waterfalls, where the water rolls over a hard magma sill in the softer surrounding limestone.

After around a kilometre you will pass a series of springs, where the water bubbles from various holes in the ground. Above this, the river bed remains obvious as a dry ribbon of washed out rocks and boulders through the landscape, but the river itself flows underground.

Further along, a fork in the path is marked by a large boulder which has been carved to point the way towards Breabag to the left, and the Bone Caves to the right. Following the right-hand fork, the path starts to rise gradually towards the crags of Creag nan Uamh - the Crag of the Caves.

There are several caves to explore along the base of the crags. All mystery and history aside, they're a great place to stop and have lunch and a flask of tea while you ponder the fact that deep within the hillside is a completely separate network of large caves that never quite link up with the Bone Caves.

To return, you can retrace your steps, or continue east around two hundred metres past the caves, where the path loops north then west to return back down the glen, rejoining the original route by the marked boulder you passed on your approach.

Parking

Grid Ref: NC 253 179

Lat/Long: 58.115472 , -4.9672823

There is a good gravel car park with space for a few vehicles signposted just off the A837, around 2.7 miles south of Inchnadamph.

Access

14km out and back.

The path is easy to follow and generally very good if uneven in places, with some short boggy sections. Some of the caves are easier to access than others, but most walkers will be able to enjoy the best of them with no difficulty.

Allt nan Uamh: Burn of the Caves
Creag nan Uamh: Rock of the Caves

Previous Page: Enjoying the view out from the Bone Caves.

Looking across to the entrance to the caves.

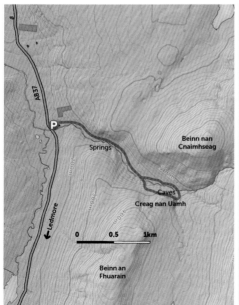

⑭ Traligill Caves

The limestone geology in Gleann Dubh has resulted in a landscape riddled with caves and tunnels. Underground rivers flow through the rocks here, and at the Traligill Caves we are allowed a tantalising glimpse of an alternate landscape beneath our feet.

These caves are very different to the Bone Caves just a few kilometres to the south. Rather than a shelter, the Traligill Caves feel like a window into the hillside. Uam an Uisge - the Cave of the Water - in particular is like a cut-away view showing the river within the rocks. Even the walk has a different atmosphere, trading the intimacy of the landscape enjoyed on the approach to the Bone Caves for more expansive views and big skies.

Most of this route is shared with walkers on the way to and from Conival and Ben More Assynt. While they test themselves against the highest summits in the area, we can enjoy the sense of discovery that the caves add to a much easier half-day walk.

The Route

From the roadside car park next to the Inchnadamph hotel, walk north along the road to cross the bridge over the River Traligill, then follow the track along the northern side of the river past the lodge houses. After around a kilometre, the track crosses a river on a small bridge next to the site of an old, abandoned township. 28 families were evicted from the area around Inchnadamph during the Highland Clearances of the early 1800s, to make way for sheep farming - a story familiar throughout much of the north west highlands.

Continue along the track, which eventually narrows to a path before splitting a few hundred metres after Glenbain Cottage. Take the right fork, signposted for Uamhan Tràiligil - The Traligill Caves.

There is a small footbridge over the River Traligill just after the path splits, and it's worth taking some time to explore the area to the right immediately after crossing it, which has some beautiful rock features and views back down the glen along an open gorge.

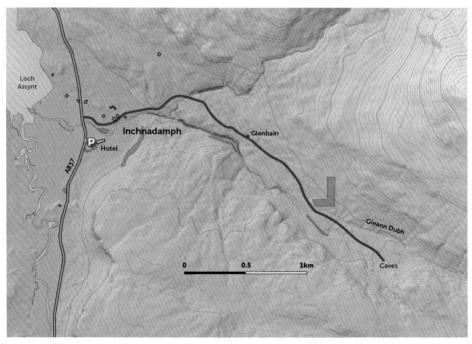

Returning to the path, you will be able to see the first of the cave openings about 600 metres ahead of you on the hillside. It is quite an incredible feature when you reach it - a narrow diagonal hole, as if the hillside has been slashed open to allow you to view the beautiful waterfall racing down the rocks beneath the surface.

This is Uamh an Uisge - the Cave of the Water - and is known locally as the "Waterslide". Light from another opening above gives you an idea of where the water arrives from, but the dark slot it vanishes into has nothing but mystery. The rock by the water is slippery, and there is no coming back should you slip into the water, so do not be tempted to climb down for a closer look.

Immediately above Uamh an Uisge is another opening - the source of the upstream light you could see from below. A third cave is found slightly up the path, and is called Uamh an Tartair - the Cave of the Roaring. Walking into the maw of this cave you will hear why, as unseen waterfalls in the dark tunnels beyond the entrance echo in the space. It is thought that the name "Traligill" may have its roots in the Norse word for Trolls, and it is easy to imagine the creatures lurking in the caves.

To return, retrace your route back to the car.

Looking down into the top of the Waterslide.

An audience on the return from the Traligill Caves.

Parking

Grid Ref: NC 251 216
Lat/Long: 58.148580 , -4.9734388

A good sized car park is just off the main A837 road in Inchnadamph, at the eastern end of Loch Assynt. Look out for the parking signpost by the Inchnadamph Hotel, immediately south of the bridge over the river Traligill. The walkers' car park is immediately off the road, before you reach the hotel.

Access

6.5km out and back.

The walking is generally straightforward, starting on access tracks and progressing to a good path. Care should be taken around the cave entrances, which can be exposed in places. Do not be tempted to enter the Waterslide cave, or to explore beyond the initial cavern of the Cave of the Roaring.

The approach to both the
Traligill Caves and Ben More Assynt.

In the late 1800s, Sir Hugh Munro compiled a list of the Scottish mountains over 3,000 feet. These 282 summits have come to be known as the "Munros", and climbing all of them is a long-term project for many walkers. There are two Munros in the Assynt area, Conival and Ben More Assynt.

These mountains may not feature on as many postcards or social media posts as Suilven, Quinag or the area's other Island Mountains, but that is purely because they lack the distinctive silhouette of their eastern contemporaries. Rest assured, an ascent of Conival and Ben More Assynt is an excellent day out! The approach is long and the climb steep, but once among the tops you will find beautiful rocky ridges above dramatic, remote coires.

This is very different in character to other mountain routes in Coigach and Assynt, but no less rewarding for it. It's a long, tiring day, but the walking is constantly interesting and the views are enough to keep a spring in your step throughout the ascent.

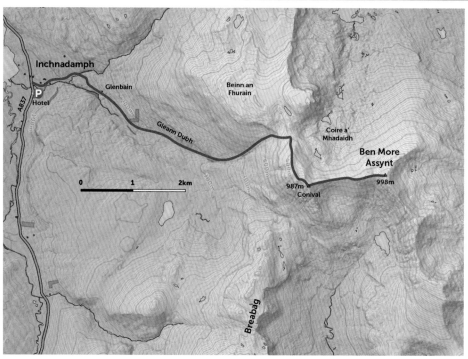

Above: Quinag and the cliffs of Na Tuadhan.
Photo: Phil Jones.

Below: Looking south over Breabag from
the slopes of Conival.

The Route

For the first 2km this route follows the path towards the Traligill Caves, which is described in detail in the previous chapter. In brief, from the car park walk north along the A837 across the bridge, then turn right onto the track leading upstream past the lodge houses. Follow the track past Glenbain Cottage until it splits by a small signpost, indicating the Traligill Caves to the right.

On this occasion we will instead take the left fork, following a smaller path along the northern bank of the Traligill river. The river and the path run along the bottom of a shallow gorge, making for a very atmospheric, intimate section of walking. After almost 2km, the path breaks left and the climb starts in earnest.

The ascent follows the Allt a' Choinnie Mhill steeply north east, and can be quite boggy in places. The burn is quite beautiful, with an endless procession of waterfalls to admire as you climb.

As the gradient eases, you are faced with a wall of rock above - a band of quartzite cliffs which requires a short section of scrambling to pass. The path leads you directly to the easiest spot to make the ascent. As you climb you might notice the white lines running through the rock. This is pipe rock, and the lines are fossilised worm burrows.

Your short scramble brings you out into an open coire, where you continue at a more sedate gradient to the bealach between Conival and Beinn an Fhurain. Turning south, the path leads you through scree and boulder fields, where the angular quartzite blocks make for a dramatic setting as you climb. The gradient relents once more as you approach the broad summit ridge of Conival, and much of the final kilometre to the first Munro is gentle enough that you can fully appreciate the epic views around you.

To the north, the pinnacles of Na Tuadhan tower above Coire a' Mhadaidh. Looking east, you have a great view along the ridge linking Conival and Ben More Assynt. To the south, you have a bird's eye view along the top of Breabag's ridge, with the sharp drop into its eastern coires making for an imposing sight.

There would be absolutely nothing wrong with calling it a day on the summit of Conival, but it is only another 3km out and back to add Ben More Assynt to your day. The ridge runs east from the summit of Conival, and includes some of the best walking of the day.

To descend, reverse the route.

Top right: walking the ridge between Ben More Assynt and Conival.

Bottom Right: the summit of Conival, with Ben More Assynt behind.

Parking

Grid Ref: NC 251 216
Lat/Long: 58.148580 , -4.9734388

A good-sized car park is just off the main A837 road in Inchnadamph, at the eastern end of Loch Assynt. Look out for the parking signpost by the Inchnadamph Hotel, immediately south of the bridge over the river Traligill. The walkers' car park is immediately off the road, before you reach the hotel.

Access

20km with 1200m ascent out and back to Ben More Assynt

This is a long, physically demanding day. The approach from Inchnadamph along Gleann Dubh is easy walking, but does add a good distance to what would already have been a tough ascent. There is a short section of scrambling to overcome the quartzite band as you ascend Conival, and difficult ground underfoot through the boulder fields along the ridges. This walk should only be considered in good weather, and by parties with sufficient experience. A map and compass should be carried.

Quinag in winter. Photo: Chris Puddephatt.

In contrast to the instantly recognisable profiles of most of the area's mountains, Quinag is a mountain of many faces. Its western wall offers little hope to walkers, with over 3km of unbroken vertical cliffs making it look more of a fortress than a mountain.

The northern aspect is little more inviting, with the great snub noses of Sàil Ghorm and Sàil Gharbh no more plausible for an ascent than the cliffs on the western flank. Here, though, at least there is the hint of a route up the coire between the two great ridges to make you think that the mountain is not completely impenetrable.

In fact, a relatively straightforward ascent to the high point can be made from the south-east. Here you'll find a very reasonably inclined ramp of quartzite slabs and heather to lead you directly, if relentlessly, from the road to the summit of Spidean Còinich.

From that top you have access to the full range of summits, ridges and coires that Quinag has to offer. Three of these summits feature in the list of Corbetts - Scottish Mountains with a height between 2500 and 3000 feet. In places the network of ridges linking them feels surprisingly delicate; narrow crests belying the massive bulk the mountain possesses when viewed from the road.

With such a complex and beautifully featured mountain, there are many options for walkers, and you can tailor your day to suit yourself. Those that venture out along ridges will undoubtedly come away with a new name on their list of favourite mountains, and the long, low fortress will never look the same again as you drive through Assynt.

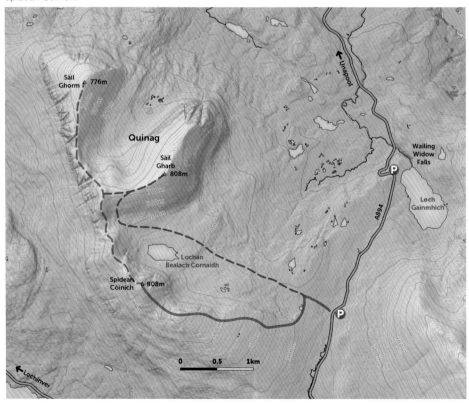

Above: arriving on the summit of Spidean Còinich.

Below: crossing the small summit after Spidean Còinich.

The Route

For all the complexities and intricacies Quinag has on offer, the route to the top of Spidean Còinich is relatively straightforward. The path starts about 50m south, across the road from the car park and strikes out west towards the Coire above. After less than 500m it splits by a cairn. Continuing straight will take you into the coire and Lochan Bealach Cornaidh.

To head for the summit, take the left fork which will lead you over rocky slabs and past a small lochan. After the lochan, swing west to climb directly towards the summit. The gradient is steady through the heather and the exposed slabs of Cambrian Quartzite that line this face of the hill. Keep your eyes open for badgers, pine marten and blue hares. Ptarmigan nest among the rocks, and there's every chance you'll see Golden Eagles soaring above.

There's a false summit at 620m, then the terrain steepens on the final approach to the actual top, which is quite beautiful - a small rocky plateau with cliffs on its northern side. After enjoying the view south over Suilven and Canisp during the climb, from here the view along Quinag's main ridge towards Sàil Ghorm and across to Sàil Gharbh now commands most of the attention.

Those wanting a (relatively) easy hill day can turn back here satisfied, but there are several options for those still hankering for more.

Continuing over the Spidean Coinich to the north-west a ridge takes you to a tiny lochan - Lochan Ruadh - on a shallow bealach before a second, slightly lower summit. Progress north from here is trickier, with a rough descent on steep ground to the Bealach a' Chornaidh. From here you have the option to descend back to the car by dropping east into the coire, where you may spend some time bog-trotting, before picking up the path to the car park.

Alternatively, you can climb steeply north to the central peak of the massif where again you have options. Continuing north towards Sàil Ghorm is a bit of an adventure, with a narrow ridge providing plenty of interest. For those that don't actively enjoy heights, heading directly east towards Sail Gharbh will be the better option, with the ridge linking the central peak and the eastern Corbett reassuringly lacking in exposure. It may be less dramatic walking, but the beautifully weathered Torridonian Sandstone slabs make it no less beautiful.

Whichever peak you opt for, the easiest route down afterwards is to return to the low spot 500m east along the ridge towards Sàil Gharb. A small cairn marks the start of a path descending south towards Lochan Bealach Cornaidh, where you will pick up the main path back to the car park.

Ptarmigan on the approach to Spidean Còinich.

Looking over Lochan Bealach Cornaidh and Spidean Còinich. Photo: Chris Puddephatt.

Access

9km with 600m ascent out and back to Spidean Còinich.

14km with 1100m ascent for all three Corbetts.

The climb to Spidean Còinich is relatively straightforward by the standards of mountain days, but walkers should be sure to carry suitable clothing and equipment. Extending the day beyond the first summit, the terrain becomes more difficult and some parts of the ridges can be quite exposed. A map and compass are essential, as the weather and visibility can change very quickly. Only attempt in winter conditions if suitably experienced and equipped with axe and crampons.

This is a mountain that captures the imagination of many. If you feel that you want to experience more than just the view from afar but are not sure you have the fitness or skill to tackle an ascent, you might consider an out-and-back walk out to Lochan Bealach Cornaidh.

Quinag is managed by the John Muir Trust. Find out more about their work online at www.JohnMuirTrust.org

Parking

Grid Ref: NC 233 274
Lat/Long: 58.199886 , -5.0083687

There is a large gravel car park with space for several cars set back off the eastern side of the main A894 road between Loch Assynt and Kylesku, about 1km south of its high point.

Ardvreck Castle, on Loch Assynt. The castle was built late in the 15th century by the MacLeods of Assynt. It was captured by the Mackenzies in 1672, who replaced it with the more modern Calda House in 1726. The ruins of both Calda House and Ardvreck Castle can be seen by the roadside as you drive around the loch.

⑰ Little Assynt Estate

The Little Assynt Estate has been in community ownership since the end of 2000. The estate covers over 2900 acres and much of it has been planted with native trees, protected from the local deer by fence. There are two excellent paths on the estate, which can be accessed individually or linked into a single longer walk.

The Loch an t-Sabhail path is a circular route, taking in several excellent viewpoints, and passing the remains of a deserted township.

In 2005 the all-abilities path was opened, providing a fantastic route through the landscape that is accessible to all, including those with prams, pushchairs or wheelchairs. There are shelters and accessible toilets by each of the two lochs the path passes. Each also has a small jetty with boats adapted for disabled anglers.

Both routes have superb views across to Quinag in particular, and you should keep your eyes open for otters and Golden Eagles. If you listen carefully you might hear the call of the Black-Throated Divers too.

The start of each of the two paths are obvious from their respective car parks. Both routes are on good paths that are very well maintained.

All-Abilities Path

As you start this route, the first of the two shelters and toilets are found after just a couple hundred metres by the side of Loch Leitir Easaidh. The second shelter and toilet are found by Loch na h-Innse Fraoich, near the start of the loop out to the viewpoint towards Suilven.

The gradient gradually increases as you approach the viewpoint, but the path remains smooth throughout. Just before you reach the top of the small rise, a footpath leads off to the west, linking this route with the Lochan t-Sabhail circuit.

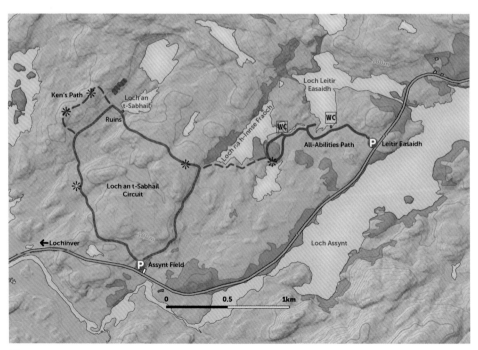

Loch an t-Sabhail Circuit

This circular route is longer than the All-Abilities path, and while not wheelchair accessible it is a good, smooth path all the way around. The views are good throughout and there are several marked viewpoints, with the option to visit a couple more if you extend the route slightly by taking in Ken's Path.

The ruins of the old township lie along the furthest stretch of the path. The remains of several tenants' houses can be seen, along with a small mill by the side of the burn.

Right: a stonechat, photographed at Little Assynt Estate.
Photo: David Haines

Below: Quinag from Little Assynt Estate.
Photo: Justine Ritchie.

Parking - All Abilities Path

Grid Ref: NC 172 262
Lat/Long: 58.186210 , -5.1101788

Parking - Loch an t-Sabhail Circuit

Grid Ref: NC 154 252
Lat/Long: 58.176481 , -5.1411246

Both car parks are located on the northern side of the main A837 road. The Loch an t-Sabhail car park is just beyond the western end of of Loch Assynt, and the Leitir Easaidh car park is around 1km west of the Loch Assynt Lodge.

Access

2.7km for the All-Abilities path.

4.5km for the Loch an t-Sabhail circuit.

Both paths are excellent, and very well maintained. The All-Abilities path is wheelchair accessible, though does have a slight gradient towards the top of the viewpoint. To book the fishing boats, visit the *Boat Hire and Permits* page on www.AssyntAngling.com.

Both the shelters on the All-Abilities path have adjacent composting toilets that are wheelchair accessible.

(18) Inver Loop

The Inver Loop is an excellent half-day walk starting and finishing in Lochinver, with loads of variety and superb views throughout. The route can be done clockwise, but is described here counter-clockwise, making most of the views over Suilven in the Lochinver to Glencanisp stage, and over Quinag later on.

Along the way you'll pass the remains of the old township of Dubh Chlais, which was abandoned in the Highland Clearances in 1812, and the Glencanisp Lodge which was previously a shooting lodge but is now owned and operated by the Assynt Foundation. The Foundation bought out the Glencanisp and Drumrunie estates in 2005, meaning that most of the land that you pass through on your walk is now in community ownership.

Autumn colour on the Inver Loop.
Photo: Chris Puddephatt.

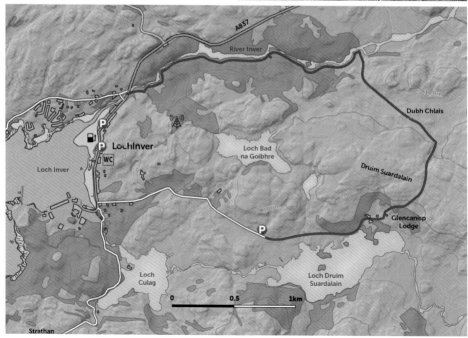

The Route

The first part of the route runs from Lochinver to the Glencanisp Lodge along a paved single-track road, starting towards the southern end of the village, immediately north of the pedestrian crossing. Follow this road for 2.5km to reach the lodge. On the way you'll pass through some nice woodland before the view opens out over Loch Druim Suardalain with Suilven in the distance.

When you reach the lodge, follow the signs to go left around the main building and past the Pole Barn. The track splits, with the right hand fork heading east towards Suilven and our route signposted for the River Inver to the left. The route goes past the new, wooden artist's studio then straight up the hill and through a gate. A short climb takes you up onto the broad ridge of Druim Suardalain, where you have a superb view back to Suilven.

Continuing north you swap the views of Suilven for Quinag, and soon reach a signpost pointing you through a kissing gate. It is here that you will see some of the remains of the Dubh Chlais township.

The River Inver.
Photo: Chris Puddephatt.

A few hundred metres past the ruins you meet the River Inver. The path follows the river back into the village and it is not unusual to see otters along the banks. Twitchers should keep an eye out for osprey hunting, as well as great-spotted woodpeckers, woodcock, treecreepers and siskins.

You will pass lots of short piers that are used by fishermen. Should you find yourself by a fisherman's hut next to a weir, you've missed the main route breaking from the river, and can rejoin it by taking the path behind the hut.

Dubh Chlais Township

The township of Dubh Chlais was home to six households when it was cleared to make way for sheep farming in 1812. The buildings are ruins today, some remain as obvious stone structures while many are now little more than mounds among the bracken. The flat areas of grass in front of the ruins were once the "corn fields" where bere barley and black oats were grown. Potatoes were grown in the old rigs, and Highland cows would have been kept for milking and producing cheese.

Above: climbing Druim Suardalain.

Right: Quinag from where the path meets the River Inver.

Parking

There are several parking options in the village of Lochinver. Starting and finishing the route in the village has the advantage of ending your walk right next to several good cafes!

Access

6.5km circular walk.

The walk starts on a quiet, paved minor road before transitioning onto good hill paths. The return leg of the walk is along a riverside path that is slightly more uneven, but which should pose no difficulty for most walkers.

In addition to the route described, there is the option of a nature trail behind the Glencanisp Lodge, which offers good views of Suilven and the Walled Garden, which is in the process of being restored. A leaflet with information on the route is available at the gate of the Lodge.

Information about fishing in the area can be found on www.assyntanglinginfo.org.uk.

Walkers on the final climb to Caisteal Liat, Suilven.
Photo: Chris Puddephatt.

There is no other mountain quite like Suilven.

It is the centrepiece of the area, and commands the landscape from every direction. With the huge dome and snub nose of Caisteal Liath and the narrow ridge leading south-east to Meall Meadhonach, the mountain has a distinct and instantly recognisable form. As you drive around Assynt it remains distant, the central hub around which everything else revolves.

Perhaps this is part of Suilven's lure... its towering ridges and dark cliffs lend it an unmistakable sense of gravitas and power, but the fact that it always seems so remote certainly seems to add to the mountain's air of mystery.

This is no trick of the landscape either; the simple fact is that Suilven is a long way from the nearest road. While not a large mountain in terms of height, the long walk to reach its base before you even begin to climb, and the tramp back out afterwards on tired legs, means that an ascent is hard earned.

It may be a long day, but there are few hill days to compare. Perhaps best of all is the sense of achievement. As hypnotic as Suilven can be when first seen, it is doubly so when viewed through the memory of a long day courting its summit. This is a mountain journey never to be forgotten.

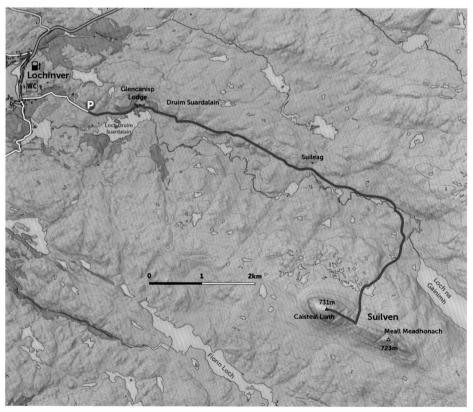

Suilven, from the approach along Glencanisp.
Photo: Chris Puddephatt.

The Route

From the walkers' car park, continue along the road to the Glencanisp Lodge where the track runs around the back of the main building. Just after the lodge, the track sweeps left up the hill, but rather than follow it you should follow the right fork at the corner signposted as the Suilven path.

This is the start of a long path that runs from here all the way through to Ledmore in the east. We will be following it for a little under half its length before breaking south to make an ascent of Suilven.

The path is good throughout its length and runs more-or-less alongside the river, which broadens into small lochans at several places. A couple of tracks break north off the main route, but continue steadfastly on your way towards the mountain. The last of these paths is marked by a cairn (NC 148 210), and a short walk along this track will take you to Suileag bothy, which is a good shelter if you're choosing to tackle the route over 2 days.

About 2.5km after the path to Suileag you cross a

wooden bridge over the river, and the path climbs slightly as it sweeps south. A little over 500m past the bridge, take the obvious path breaking right, directly towards the mountain.

Suilven disappears from view briefly as you climb steeply towards the broad, lochan-speckled terrace at the base of the mountain. When you arrive, the broad flank of the hill feels very close indeed, and the place definitely has an imposing atmosphere. The horizontal banding of the sandstone layers is split by huge vertical cracks and gullies, making the dome of Caisteal Liath seem like it was assembled from huge blocks. You'll see the path to the bealach snaking up the side of the hill, looking for all the world as if it is completely vertical.

After skirting around the western side of Loch a' Choire Dubh to reach the climb, you'll remember this thought, for as short as the climb may be it is relentlessly steep on legs already weary from the approach.

On reaching the bealach, you immediately have a grand view across the mountains to the south and once you catch your breath any suffering involved in reaching here is forgotten. Cùl Mòr and Cùl Beag are almost directly to the south, and Stac Pollaidh looks superb across Loch Sionasgaig, with the broad massif of Ben More Coigach beyond.

Turning north-west to head towards the summit, you will pass a very beautiful old wall that runs perpendicular to the ridge. From here, the summit is less than 500m distant, and the final approach has just enough easy scrambling to make it a little bit of an adventure. It is a fitting way to arrive at the top of one of the most magnificent mountains in the country!

The summit itself is quite spacious, and has pretty incredible views in every direction. Not least of these is looking back south-east along the ridge, past the bealach towards Meall Meadhonach - the "tail" of Suilven. The walk out over Meall Meadhonach to Meall Beag at the far end of the ridge involves some slightly trickier scrambling, and greater exposure than the walk to the summit of Caisteal Liath.

To return, retrace your route back to the lodge, and the car park beyond.

Walkers on the bealach.
Photo: Tim Hamlet.

Access

22km with 950m ascent out and back.

The ascent of Suilven itself is not particularly difficult or complex, but the approach is long and the distances involved make this a long and physically arduous day. The paths are good throughout, though the climb to the bealach is very steep. Some limited, easy scrambling is needed to reach the summit from the bealach, but unless you're actively afraid of heights it is not likely to be a problem.

An ascent is often done over two days, with a wild camp or a stay at Suileag bothy to split the journey (the bothy can be popular, so take a tent in case it's full). Carrying camping kit means a heavier load, so it is debatable whether this makes things easier, but a remote camp is undoubtedly a memorable experience. A solid, lightweight mountain tent is essential if planning a high camp, and you should pay heed to the weather forecast. Even modest winds at sea level can be surprisingly powerful on the summit or along the ridge, and there are many stories of tents being destroyed up there. If in doubt, camp below the mountain.

Parking

Grid Ref: NC 107 220
Lat/Long: 58.146234 , -5.2180091

There is a walkers' car park on the Glencanisp road. The road starts towards the southern end of Lochinver, just north of the road to Inverkirkaig. The parking area is around 1km before the Lodge. If the walkers' car park is full, the only alternative is to park in the village and walk in.

Clouds brewing on the ridge.
Photo: Chris Puddephatt.

⓴ Culag Woods

A walk in the woods can be like a hug from nature. There's something about being among the trees that calms the soul and relaxes us like nowhere else.

The Culag Community Woods have a great network of accessible paths, and are the perfect place to get some "tree time." With a sculpture trail and plenty of good dens and hides to discover, it is a great family day out too. Also keep an eye open for the nature trail, marked by numbered posts, and the orienteering course which is marked by carved leaves. The "Are You Brave Enough?" trail where the kids can have a bit of an adventure!

The Route

The Culag Woods can be accessed directly from Lochinver but there are also two car parks that service the woods directly. There are several paths through the woods, and they are all well signposted.

Each path has its own character. The main path through the woods runs through the heart of the forest, linking the two car parks, and is broad, smooth and well drained.

The path up to the viewpoint is steeper, narrower and a little more uneven. Once at the summit, a bench looks out across Lochinver to the north.

Below Right: Black Darter dragonfly on Bog Myrtle. Photo: David Haines.

Continue a little further past the first view and you have a superb view out to the prow of Suilven, one of the most beautiful mountains in Scotland.

At the south-west corner of the woods is White Shore. This is one of the best picnic spots in the area, with benches among the trees and even a couple of rope swings from the branches. The pebble beach is nice and sheltered, and a great spot to watch the boats coming and going from Lochinver harbour.

Billy's Path links the area near White Shore directly with the western end of Lochinver harbour - it's a narrower path than others in the woods, and has a great picnic bench. Billy's Path can also be accessed from Lochinver harbour, just past the Lifeboat and Coastguard buildings.

Things to See

The woods are full of life! If you're lucky you might catch sight of otters and pine martens, or the heron that nest in the treetops here. There are over a hundred kinds of flowering plants in the woods, and the mosses and lichens thrive in the clean air. In the autumn, see how many different kinds of fungi you can spot. There's also an impressive range of sculptures to find as you explore, with dens and shelters to hide in along the way!

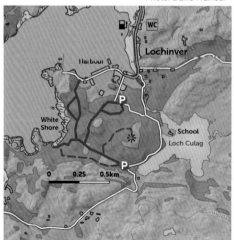

One of the shelters in the Culag Woods.
Photo: Mairi-Anne MacLeod.

Parking

Main Car Park
Grid Ref: NC 092 220
Lat/Long: 58.145432 , -5.2425840

Alternate Car Park
Grid Ref: NC 093 215
Lat/Long: 58.140692 , -5.2416428

There are two car parks at opposite ends of the woods. Both are accessed from the minor road south from Lochinver, heading towards Inverkirkaig. The first is found along an unpaved track marked by a wooden sign halfway up the hill to the local school. The other is roadside, about a kilometre south of the village, just past the end of Loch Culag.

The woods can also be accessed on foot from the southern end of Lochinver, by following the road past An Cala Cafe, or meeting the end of Billy's Path just beyond the lifeboat and Coastguard building at the harbour.

Access

The paths are all good, well maintained and easy walking, although wet days can make them slippy, particularly in autumn when there are leaves on the ground. Some will be accessible for buggies and prams, and the woods make for an excellent day out with young family. Leaflets with maps of the paths are available in both car parks.

㉑ Inverkirkaig to Fionn Loch

This walk along the River Kirkaig has a little bit of everything. The initial stages of the walk lead through beautiful woodland, climbing to give superb views across to Stac Pollaidh, Cùl Mor and Cùl Beag as the river flows below you in a steep gorge. The short detour to visit the Falls of Kirkaig is a must, but it is arguably the views across Fionn Loch towards Suilven at the farthest point of the walk that will remain with you for longest.

Most of the walk feels quite intimate as you track up the River Kirkaig below the lip of its broad, open gorge. On reaching Fionn Loch the view expands dramatically before you, making the view of Suilven feel like a real event; the curtain suddenly drawn back to allow you an audience with the mighty centrepiece of Assynt.

The path continues from here, leading all the way to the mountain itself. While any day spent climbing Suilven is a day well spent, the approach from here is long and very boggy in places. For those that want to tackle an ascent, we have instead described the approach from Glencanisp - see page 94.

The Route

The route starts along the lower, right hand track across from the car park, initially following an access road to a private house.

A plaque holds an inscription of the poem "Climbing Suilven" by Normal McCaig. As the road turns left towards the house, take the walkers' path through on the outside of the bend.

The path climbs gently alongside the river as it tumbles and weaves through woods of hazel, birch, rowan, aspen and holly. Redpolls, Willow Warblers and Tree Pipits can be spotted, and in the spring the forest floor hosts primrose, wood sorrel, Wood Anemone and dog violets. Slowly, the trees thin and you climb above the river as the gorge walls steepen.

After 3km you reach a fork, with the right hand path signposted for the Falls of Kirkaig. The falls are only a few minutes detour, and absolutely worth a visit - just be careful on the steep rocks above the river, particularly if they're wet.

You will have your first clear views of Suilven just a couple of hundred metres after rejoining the main path. Fionn Loch is about 1km beyond the falls, and out on the open hillside here you may hear the cuckoo calling or see stonechat in the whin bushes.

Reverse your route to return to Inverkirkaig, where you can reward yourself with a stop at the cafe next to the car park.

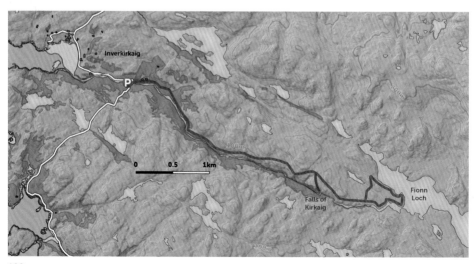

Cùl Mor, Cùl Beag and Stac Pollaidh from the walk along the River Kirkaig.

Parking

Grid Ref: NC 085 193
Lat/Long: 58.121546 , -5.2523026

From Lochinver, drive south on the minor road signposted for Inverkirkaig for 2.5 miles. There is a large car park next to the river.

The road continues all the way through to Coigach in the south, but be aware that it is very narrow and the passing places are irregularly spaced. Larger vehicles should avoid continuing beyond Inverkirkaig.

Access

9km out and back to Fionn Loch.

The path is easy to follow but can be quite uneven underfoot in places. There is a shallow, steady climb for the entire outward leg. The viewpoint for the falls is quite exposed, and care should be taken on the rocks, particularly if they are wet. Bear in mind that the start of the route is essentially along someone's driveway - please be considerate.

There is a cafe right next to the car park, just up the drive to the left of the start of the route.

Blooming heather, and Suilven over Fionn Loch, photographed after a summer sunset.

Achmelvich is a wonderful place to arrive by any means, yet there's something particularly satisfying about getting there under your own steam. This walk from Lochinver is the perfect route for those wanting to make the most of their journey to one of Scotland's most beautiful bays.

The walk has a little of everything, from expansive views across Loch Inver and Suilven, to an intimate walk among the cnocs and small lochans. Buzzards are a common sight, and peregrines are often spotted along the route. As you drop down to the head of Loch Roe you might be lucky enough to glimpse an otter, and there are normally seals.

Of course, perhaps best of all is that at the end of the walk you're at Achmelvich, where the machair blooms brilliant yellow in the summer and the marram dunes dance in the wind all year round.

The water here is a brilliant blue green that may look more tropical than it feels, but don't let that put you off taking a dip! A pod of Harbour Porpoise often visit in the summer, and dolphins and whales aren't uncommon.

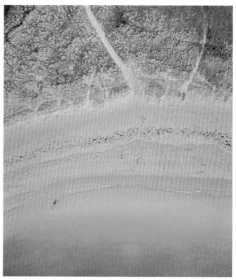

Perfect white sand, and beautiful green water at Achmelvich beach.

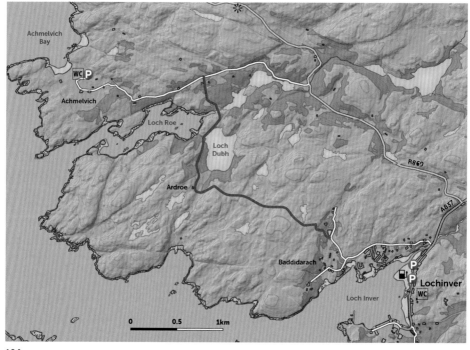

Looking back to Lochinver and the mountains.

The Route

The first stretch of this walk takes you around the northern side of Lochinver. Cross the stone bridge over the river at the head of the loch, then walk west towards the Highland Stoneware pottery and Baddidarach. One kilometre from the bridge, take the right hand fork in the road to go up the hill, followed by the left fork a couple hundred metres later. A hand-written sign at the end of a driveway will point you in the right direction before the official sign directs you left through a gate.

At this point you are among the trees, but as they quickly give way to open hillside you should be sure to pause to enjoy the view back over Lochinver. The huge dome of Suilven looks deceptively close on a clear day, appearing to tower over the village nestling on the shore.

The path meanders through the Lewisian Gneiss landscape for one and a half kilometres before reaching the crofts at Ardroe. A beautiful old wall lines one side of the path as you approach, with the remains of old croft buildings half buried at the base of the crags on the other side. The path meets the croft access road just past the end of the wall. The track will lead you past the banks

of Loch Dubh and down to a bridge over the river between Lochan Sàile and Loch Roe.

Otters are sometimes seen here, and common seals are normally found on the rocks along the water's edge. The seals are often more easily spotted from above, after you've followed the (now paved) road up to join with the single-track road to Achmelvich. Turn left onto the road when you reach it. The road can see some traffic on a good summer's day, but the views over Loch Roe make it a very pleasant walk.

You will pass a line of homes and caravan parks as you arrive in Achmelvich, with a couple of small shops to provide refreshments and souvenirs. Then the machair gives way to the marram dunes, which in turn release you onto perfect white sands overlooking emerald waters. West of the beach, the An Fharaid Bhead peninsula is a lovely place to explore, with the Hermit's Castle waiting to be discovered.

You can continue your walk out to the old mill at Alltannabradhan, as described in the next chapter. Or you can just find a quiet spot to sit... somewhere to enjoy the tranquility of the sheltered bay and make the most of some quiet time.

Achmelvich Bay.

The Machair: *fertile, low grassy plain.*

Machair is one of the rarest habitats in Europe, and is unique to the islands and west coasts of Scotland and Ireland. White sand beaches tend to be made from calcium-rich particles of broken down shells, and when they are washed or blown inland they fertilise the soil. The calcium makes the area alkaline, often in areas that are otherwise quite acidic, like much of our peat-clad coast. In some places, light grazing by livestock and low intensity farming over many generations has helped make the machair what it is today.

In the summer months the machair can be a riot of colour, its hue shifting as different flowers come into season. Birds-foot Trefoil and Lady's Bedstraw can make the machair at Achmelvich almost pure yellow. You might also find Autumn Gentian, Fairy Flax, Spring Squill and Wild Carrot. As the machair transitions into the surrounding heather, look for pink fragrant orchids, butterfly orchids and the rare Pyramidal Bugle.

Sunset from the sands at Achmelvich.

Parking

Grid Ref: NC 094 227
Lat/Long: 58.151953 , -5.2406275

The route starts from Lochinver, where there are a couple of car parks along the main road. Public toilets are also available just south of the police station.

Access

6.5km one way.

Starting and finishing on paved roads and with a good path and track in between, this is a straightforward route. Shops, cafes and public toilets are available at both ends of the route (though the shops and cafe may be closed at Achmelvich outside the high season). This is described as a one-way route so you'll want someone to meet you at the far end, or you can reverse the route to return to Lochinver.

It's no exaggeration to say that Achmelvich is among the most beautiful beaches in the country. Pristine white sands, low marram dunes and acres of beautiful machair combine to make the place perfectly idyllic.

This is a beautiful short walk from Achmelvich to the remains of an old mill at Altanabradhan. The picture-perfect beach and caravan park at Achmelvich have made it a popular destination, but you don't have to walk far before you feel like you are alone in the landscape.

Before you go, or perhaps after you return, be sure to explore the beautiful features around Achmelvich itself. The main beach is unmissable, but a second little cove is accessible from a little way along the Altananbradhan path. In the other direction, the headland of An Fharaid Bheag to the west of the main beach is a lot of fun to explore, and has one of Scotland's oddest little "castles" hidden away among its rocky inlets.

The Route

From the car park, the walk starts along a gravel track leading to a small crofting township, clearly signposted for Altanabradhan. Soon after you start the walk, you will see a hint of a beautiful little bay down to the left, which can be reached by a sandy little scramble down a narrow path. This is a beautiful place for a swim, and a little more secluded than the main beach - it also has some of the most beautifully featured Lewisian Gneiss in the area, with incredible colours running through the complex folds and waves in the rock.

Continuing towards the mill, you will see a path signposted for Alltananbradhan split left off the track as you approach a cluster of croft houses. Following it, you will weave through the cnocs and lochans landscape that makes Assynt special, and in a remarkably short distance will likely have the place almost to yourself.

The route is well signposted as it passes a small group of holiday cottages, with the path going left around the garden of the main house. From here you are almost at the remains of the old mill. There is no mistaking it when you first see it - old millstones lie at the outflow of the stream from the ruins, and more serve as stepping stones over the small burn you cross to reach it.

From the mill, there is a path leading down to Port Alltan na Bradhan, where low tide exposes a nice little beach, perfect for a swim. The path can also be followed inland along the burn to reach the road, but it is much more pleasant to return by reversing your outward route.

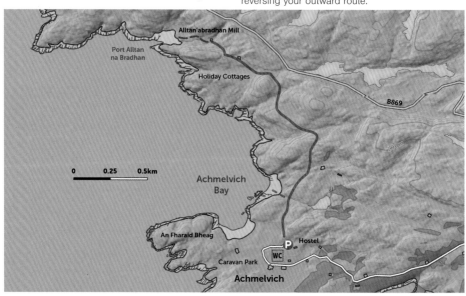

*Above: looking back towards Achmelvich
and the An Fharaid Bheag peninsula.*

Below: the sheltered cove near the start of the walk.

Beautifully folded Lewisian Gneiss.
Photo: Mairi-Anne MacLeod.

Parking

Grid Ref: NC 059 248
Lat/Long: 58.169259 , -5.3017378

Less than a kilometre north out of Lochinver, the B869 turns towards Achmelvich, Clachtoll and Stoer. 2 kilometres along this road, the turn for Achmelvich road is well signposted. The car park is at the far end of a narrow single-track road. This is a popular spot, and if the car park is full please resist the urge to park in the passing-places on the final stretch of the road through the machair.

Access

3.5km out and back.

There are sheep and ponies present along most of the route, so please close any gates you pass, and keep dogs on leads. The path is good, and shouldn't pose any particular difficulties. The ranger's station has more information about the local geology and recent wildlife sightings. There are public toilets at the car park - those at the campsite are for residents only. Through the summer season, the site shop and food van are open to all visitors.

The Old Mill

The mill at Altanabradhan was built around the 19th century. Mills like this were known as Clack Mills, due to the sound that they made. They were powered by water turning wooden paddles, which in turn rotated one of the millstones. A dam and sluice at Loch na Creige Lèithe - the Loch of the Grey Crag - was used to control the water flow at Altanabradhan.

Local lore says that John MacLeod wanted the hardest stone he could find for the millstones here, which he took from Caisteal Laith on Suilven. He cut and dressed the stones on the mountain, before carrying them down to the coast at Inverkirkaig, where he put them in a boat to transport them to Port Alltan na Bradhan, just below the mill. When you see Suilven on the horizon on the walk back from the mill, you'll appreciate the effort this must have taken!

Millstones at the outflow of the Altanabradhan Mill.

Am Bàthadh

Cha b' e tubaist a bh' ann:
's ann a dh'èirich an sàl
beag air bheag,
a' falach creagan nan Cruithneach,
a' lobhadh nan sgothan Lochlainneach,
ag èaladh tro mhachair nan Gàidheal,
blàth air bhlàth a' dol fodha,
sligean maoraich is cnàmhan dhaoine
a' tighinn gu chèile,
aonadh a' tighinn à dealachadh
is saorsa
a' call a leus anns a' chamhanaich.

Ach air cho saorsainneach 's tha feallsanachd
is air cho stèidhichte 's tha eachdraidh,
's air cho taiceil 's a tha creideamh,
nuair a chì thu an fhairge ag èirigh,
's mar a chaidh creagan 'nan sprùilleach,
's an cop romhad 's air do chùlaibh,
bu cho math dhut bhith gun dùil ri
aiseirigh:
tiodhlaic do dhòchas ri àl eile.

Ruaraidh MacThòmais

Submerging

It wasn't an accident:
the sea level rose
little by little,
hiding the Picts' rocks,
rotting the Norse skiffs,
edging through the Gaels' machair,
blossom after blossom being submerged,
shellfish shells and human bones
intermingling,
union coming from separation
and freedom
losing its sheen in the dusk.

No matter how redemptive philosophy is,
how established history,
how supportive religion,
when you see the ocean rising,
with rocks turned to rubble,
with foam before you, behind you,
you might as well not expect
renewal:
pass on your hope to another generation.

Derick Thomson

The Salmon Bothy and Split Rock, Clachtoll.

This is one of the shorter walks in the guidebook, and rather than a set route it's better to consider it a collection of places to explore in and around Clachtoll.

Everything here starts and finishes with the beautiful sandy beach, backed by classic marram grass dunes and machair. From there you get a great view across to Split Rock, which is all the more impressive on a stormy day when the waves crashing over it. There's also the old Salmon Bothy, complete with the poles where the nets were hung to dry.

For those with an interest in the local history, perhaps the most fascinating features are found after a short walk around the coast to the Bay of Stoer. Here you'll find the spectacular remains of a 2000 year old broch, built in the iron age and recently excavated by Historic Assynt. Less obvious, but irresistible to anyone with an interest in geology, is a walk to Stac Fada, where the rocks tell the tale of a meteor strike millions of years ago.

"Frankenstein's Stitches", seen in the rocks on Clachtoll beach.

The Beach

The route from the car park to the beach is quite obvious, and there are a couple of wooden walkways over the marram dunes to help you reach the sandy shore without damaging the grasses. Once there, you'll be treated to brilliant white sands and blue-green waters. On a calm day this is a perfect place for a swim, and on a stormy day the waves pick up quickly and can be very impressive.

There is a rocky outcrop of Torridonian Sandstone in the middle of the beach. Look out for "Frankenstein's Stitches", where tiny cracks formed when the mud - which eventually became the sandstone rock - first dried out some 1200 million years ago. Over time, the sea has smoothed and eroded the exposed edges of the cracks to look eerily like the scars of Shelly's unfortunate monster.

South of the main beach, near a small cove that gets cut off by the high tide, you'll also find a line in the rocks where the Torridonian Sandstone meets the much older Lewisian Gneiss. There is about 500 million years of time separating the formation of these rocks, and finding them right next to each other like this is called an "unconformity".

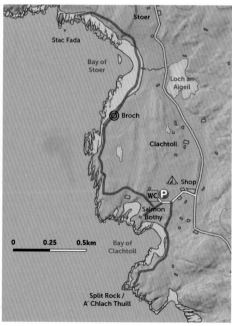

Marram grass weaving in the wind at Clachtoll.

To Split Rock

Clachtoll's split rock is such an iconic feature that it has been adopted as the logo for the Assynt Crofters' Trust. The rock may once have been attached to the cliff above, before sliding down the natural bedding plane of the rocks to its current position. Another theory is that the gap was once the tunnel beneath a natural rock arch which eventually collapsed.

Local lore tells us that Kenneth MacKenzie - known as the Brahan Seer - had prophesied that the rock would fall, and that it would be so loud that the cattle belonging to a farmer in Ledmore, 20 miles away, would take fright. The story is that on the day the rock fell the same cattle had been brought to the shore at Clachtoll, and the prophesy was realised.

From the north-eastern corner of the beach it is easy to step up to walk along the top of the rocks, heading south for a closer look at Split Rock. A gate in the fence will let you into a crofter's field briefly, to pass an otherwise difficult section of the rocks along the way. There is an excellent view of the unconformity from above if you continue about 15m past the gate, before doubling back to continue to Split Rock.

A stile takes you back out onto the start of the headland, near a path down to a beautiful sandy cove, and you can see more of the unconformity from the sand at low tide. Crossing the grass, you'll notice lots of pronounced ridges, which are old "lazy beds", where kelp was piled up to help fertilise the ground for growing crops. They are common on the west coast and islands, but the ones here are among the most pronounced in Assynt. Once you reach them, it is only a short walk south-west to the Split Rock.

The unconformity - Torridonian Sandstone and Lewisian Gneiss.

Clachtoll Salmon Bothy.

The Salmon Bothy

The Salmon Bothy can be reached directly from the car park, or by scrambling up the steep embankment at the north-western end of the beach and crossing a small stile. The bothy was built in 1846 and used by fishermen until as late as 1994, the tall poles alongside used to hang the nets to dry. The building now hosts a small museum which is open through the summer season, and worth a visit.

The view from the bothy gives one of the best vantages of Split Rock.

Clachtoll Broch

From the bothy, walk north-west following the path next to the croft access road. This will take you to a memorial to the Reverend Norman MacLeod, who led many Highlanders to new homes on distant shores during the clearances. There is a similar stone to commemorate him in Nova Scotia, and a museum in New Zealand.

From the memorial, go through the green gate with the cheery "walkers welcome" sign, then cross the road diagonally to the left to go through another gate. Follow the path along the wall through the croft before a final gate takes you out onto open fields. Follow the path as it cuts west before sweeping north along the coast towards the broch, about 600m distant.

The broch was excavated by Historic Assynt in 2017, removing the rubble that collapsed into the centre of the building and revealing a lot of the surviving detail. You'll be able to see the twin outer walls of the broch, and some of the chambers and stairs that wound upwards between them. Before its collapse, the tower would have stood around 10m high with several internal floors - a huge structure for its time.

Clachtoll broch has been dated to between 150BC and 50AD, and while it's clear that they were lived in, exactly why such extravagant structures were built remains something of a mystery.

Clachtoll Broch from above.

Stac Fada

From the broch you have a clear view north along the stoney beach of Stoer Bay. At the far end of the bay you will see layers of rock running diagonally down the hillside into the sea. Near the end of one of the sloping terraces is a small rock, known as Stac Fada. It might look perfectly ordinary from a distance, but this modest rock marks a layer of ejecta from a meteor strike.

Meteor ejecta above Stac Fada.

The gently sloping terraces can be reached by scrambling around the rocks at low tide, but it is easier to follow the path along the grass above, then drop down to the rocks once you are in line with Stac Fada. The layer you are looking for is not instantly obvious, but if you examine the rocks carefully you will find a broad band of sandstone which contains a dark green rock mixed through it.

Recent research suggests that the meteor may have struck inland near Lairg. Some scientists still think that the impact was more likely to have been out in the Minch - hopefully more research in coming years might help solve the puzzle!

To return to Clachtoll, retrace your outward route.

An aerial view taking in Split Rock, the beach, campsite and even the Bay of Stoer in the distance.

Parking

Grid Ref: NC 040 273
Lat/Long: 58.190836 , -5.3360800

Take the turn onto the B869 signposted for Achmelvich and Clachtoll, just north out of Lochinver. Clachtoll lies just over 5 miles along the single-track road. The public car park is at the end of the track through the campsite.

Access

1km out and back to Split Rock.

3km out and back to the Broch.

5km out and back to Stac Fada.

The best thing to do at Clachtoll is meander at your leisure and visit the sites that capture your attention or imagination. The walking is easy throughout, though be careful if exploring the rocks around Stac Fada.

There are public toilets in the car park, along with a ranger station that has information about the local geology and recent wildlife sightings, which can include dolphins, porpoise, whales and otters. The campsite here is excellent, and often has a food van in the summer months. There is also a great wee shop on the "main" road, Flossie's, where you can restock on groceries or grab some lunch and a hot drink.

Sheep are present in most areas described, so dogs should be kept on a lead.

The Old Man of Stoer, seen from the Point of Stoer.

25 Old Man of Stoer

There are several "Old Men" around Scotland, but we like to think that the Old Man of Stoer is the best of the lot. Everything about a visit to meet him combines to make about as satisfying a day out as you'll find anywhere.

Starting by the Stoer lighthouse, the clifftop walk has stunning views across the Minch to Lewis and Harris. Dolphins, porpoise and even whales are often seen in the waters below the cliffs. Eagles are regular visitors in the air above. There is plenty more besides to please those that enjoy spotting wildlife.

Around 2km into the walk you will quite suddenly get your first sight of the sea stack known as the Old Man. From here, the 60m pillar of beautifully weathered Torridonian Sandstone does indeed look just like an old man, posture slightly hunched as he stands off the mainland as if chatting to a friend on the clifftops of the point.

The Route

The way to the Old Man is signposted from the car park at the lighthouse. The path comes and goes - at times obvious and in places splitting into several smaller trails or fading altogether. Following the line of the clifftops will take you in the right direction. The ground is often very wet and can be slippy, so stay well back from the cliff edge.

After around a kilometre, some rough stone steps will help you cross a steep little gully. Another kilometre will see you arrive at a viewpoint looking north-east along the cliffs below Sithean Mòr, the big fairy hill, towards the Old Man himself. He looks deceptively small from here.

For a shorter day, you can turn back now, satisfied that you've seen one of the finest sea stacks in Scotland. If you have the energy, however, it is well worth the effort to continue north along the coast to reach the clifftop by the stack. Standing directly opposite him, he no longer seems quite so small. If you're lucky there might even be a group of climbers tackling the route to his summit - not a climb for the faint hearted!

If you're still hungry for more, another 500m easy walking will take you out to the Point of Stoer, where you'll find some of the best views of the Old Man, but also east towards Eddrachillis Bay and the far north-west coast of Scotland.

To return, either reverse your route, or you can opt for a route back over the high-point of the peninsula. To do so, turn inland from the highest point above the cliffs and head directly towards the summit of Sidhean Mòr. From there, continue across to the radio mast on Sidhean Beag, where you'll find a track leading back south-west to the car park. This option gives you a great view of the mountains on your return walk.

Where's he from?

The Old Man was probably formed when the sea eroded a cave out of less resistant rock. Over time the cave would have become a tunnel through the headland, forming a natural arch as the passage widened and the roof got higher. When the last of the roof finally collapsed, what had once been the seaward wall of the cave remained as a stack. The Old Man is already narrow near his base. Eventually, he too will fall.

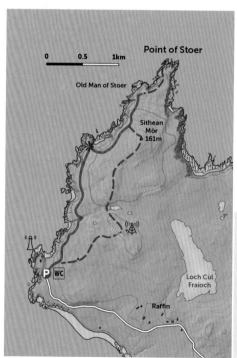

Below: Minke Whale, photographed from Stoer Lighthouse. Photo: David Haines

Above: Gannets (left), and Fulmar (right), photographed near Stoer Lighthouse. Photos: David Haines.

Wildlife at Stoer

A walk to the Point of Stoer isn't just about the Old Man. This is a great walk for spotting wildlife, both in the sea and the sky, and it's well worth taking a pair of binoculars. Keep your eyes open for:

In the water:

- Minke whales
- Orca
- Common and Risso's dolphins
- Harbour porpoises
- Grey seals
- Otters

In the sky, or nesting on the cliffs:

- Shags
- Fulmars
- Kittiwakes
- Black guillemots
- Razorbills
- Ravens
- Peregrine falcons
- Great skuas
- Puffins don't breed on the cliffs here but can sometimes be seen over the water before they fly to Handa

Looking back to the lighthouse from the path to the Old Man.

Parking

Grid Ref: NC 005 327
Lat/Long: 58.237682, -5.4001339

From Lochinver, follow the B869 past Achmelvich and Clachtoll. A mile north of the Stoer township, follow the signpost down a small single-track road towards the Point of Stoer, then signs for the Lighthouse. This car park can get very busy in high season, so please try to park considerately.

The *Loo at the Lighthouse* has become almost an attraction in its own right since it was opened in 2013. The loo is community-run, dry composting and wheelchair accessible.

Access

6km out and back to the Old Man.

8km out to the Point and back over the hilltop.

The walking generally isn't difficult, though the path can be very wet and slippy in places, and often slopes towards the edge of the cliffs. With that in mind, stay well back from the edge, particularly on windy days when powerful gusts can come from nowhere.

Sheep are regularly chased over the cliff edge by dogs, so all dogs should be kept on a lead at all times.

The first view of the Old Man on the approach.

This walk feels a little different to most in the book. This is an intimate affair, with the broader views of the mountains relegated to a supporting role. A walk along the Drumbeg and Culkein Drumbeg Peat Roads is all about atmosphere and ambience, and it has both in spades. It is an opportunity to become more familiar with the low-lying cnocs and lochans landscape that covers so much of Coigach and Assynt.

In removing the distraction of the distant view, our immediate surroundings become all the more vivid and full of detail. You'll pass several beautiful little lochans as the route picks its way through the small rises and hollows carved from the Lewisian Gneiss. Heather blooms in the summer, as do Tormentil, Heath Spotted-orchids and countless other wildflowers. Gold-ringed and Four Spot Chaser dragonflies fly low alongside the stonechats, Meadow Pipits and wheatears, while buzzards, ravens and occasionally eagles circle overhead.

These peat roads may not be as dramatic as a traverse of Quinag or as iconic as a day on Suilven, but as you return to the car after your walk, we wager you'll feel a little lighter in your step and a shade more content at heart.

The Route

Start east along the road from the viewpoint in Drumbeg. After passing the hotel, there is a crossroads, of a fashion. You should follow the lower road to the right, where there is a signpost for the Drumbeg Peat Road after 20m. Go through the gate and along the track leading past the Tea Garden.

Follow the track as it weaves its way south around various cnocs and small lochans. The Drumbeg Peat Road runs all the way to Loch Bad na Labhairt, and a simple out-and-back walk to this lochan is as good an option for a walk as any. If you would like to make a circular walk then you need to cut west across to meet the Culkien Drumbeg Peat Road for your return north.

To do this, keep an eye open for a small cairn on the right hand side of the track around 200m before you reach Loch Bad na Labhairt (NC 120 305). You'll be able to see the loch ahead of you. The cairn marks the start of the path linking the two peat roads. It can be a little vague in places, but isn't too hard to follow, and meets the Drumbeg Culkein road just after a small, unnamed lochan.

The walk north is straightforward. The landscape feels a little more expansive than it did on the outward leg, and you are afforded occasional views of the mountains peeking over the cnocs, as if to gently remind you that the rest of the world still exists before you rejoin the minor road. When you reach the road, turn right and the final mile east to the viewpoint finishes the walk off nicely.

Above: an aerlial view from the Drumbeg Peat Road.

Opposite Page: a male Wheatear near Drumbeg.
Photo: David Haines.

Parking

Grid Ref: NC 120 329
Lat/Long: 58.244535 , -5.2047585

Drumbeg lies along the very narrow, very windy little single-track road between Stoer and Unapool. Parts of the road are also very steep, and if you're in a larger mobile home this might be one to miss. The car park for the walk is at the signposted viewpoint above Loch Drumbeg, looking over Cùl Eilean and Eilean an Achaidh. Public toilets are located about 30m east along the road.

Access

7.5km circular walk.

There are sheep and occasionally highland cattle found along this route, particularly along the Drumbeg Culkein peat road, and dogs should be kept on a lead. The two peat roads are easy walking, with just a few muddy patches along the Drumbeg road. The path linking the two is easily missed (if you reach the end of the road, retrace your steps), and once on it, can be a bit vague in places. There is also one low fence to cross on this path, which at the time of writing has no stile.

125

Further Reading

We hope that this guide has helped you discover more of Coigach and Assynt, but also that it has helped you gain a little insight into the geology, history and culture that makes the area special. If you're interested in learning more about these subjects, or would like to read work inspired by or from the area, then the list below is an excellent place to start.

Between Mountain and Sea
By Norman McCaig. Norman McCaig may have lived in Edinburgh, but his heart was in Assynt. The area features strongly in his work, and he has a knack for expressing beautifully what we all feel when exploring the landscape.

The work of Mandy Haggith
Mandy Haggith is a local author and poet. She lives in Achmelvich, and teaches Literature and Creative Writing at the University of the Highlands and Islands. Mandy has published poetry collections, a tree poetry anthology, a non-fiction book about paper, and five novels, including an Iron Age historical trilogy, The Stone Stories, set at Clachtoll broch. www.mandyhaggith.net

The work of Malcolm Bangor-Jones
Malcolm is a local historian and has helped with some of the information in this guidebook. He has several books of his own, including Historic Assynt, and The Assynt Clearances.

The Assynt Crofter - Allan MacRae, A Life
By Judith Ross Napier. A biography of Allan MacRae, who was instrumental in the Assynt Crofters' Trust land buy-out in 1993.

We Have Won The Land
The story of the purchase of the Assynt Crofters' Trust of the North Lochinver Estate. By John MacAskill.

Hutton's Arse
By M.H. Rider and Peter Harrison. Coigach and Assynt feature heavily in this excellent layman's guide to geology, which describes how the rocks of Scotland helped Hutton and other pioneers develop the modern theories of the science. One of the authors, Peter Harrison, works for the North West Highlands Geopark.

Wanderings by the Lochs and Streams of Assynt and the North West Highlands of Scotland (Classic Reprint). By Hicks. A historical account of visiting Assynt.

A History of Scotland's Landscapes
By Fiona Watson. This beautiful book is a guide to reading the landscape, and finding clues about our history in what we see around us every day.

The Unremembered Places
By Patrick Baker. A collection of beautifully written essays about the joy of discovering places that have slipped from the common memory. Includes a visit to the Bone Caves at Inchnadamph.

Exploring the Landscapes of Assynt
By the NWH Geopark and British Geological Survey. This is another walking guidebook to Assynt, and while most of the routes are included in the Walker's Guide to Coigach and Assynt, it goes into much more detail in describing the geology that you will encounter on each walk.

The work of Frank Fraser Darling
Darling lived on the Summer Isles, and wrote texts about crofting in the 1950s.

Useful Websites & Contributor Links

North West Highlands Geopark
nwhgeopark.com
Find out more about the incredible geology that helps make Coigach and Assynt such a unique and beautiful place. Be sure to check out the Rock Stop visitor centre and cafe in Unapool, where you can pick up a Pebble Routes pack describing six routes taking in some of the best viewpoints and key locations in the Geopark.

Scottish Wildlife Trust
scottishwildlifetrust.org.uk
Leaders in conservation in Scotland, with an excellent range of projects around the country, including the Ben Mor Coigach reserve, near Achiltibuie.

Coigach & Assynt Living Landscape
coigach-assynt.org
Our own website, with information about our projects, past and present.

Visit Coigach
coigach.com
Information about the Coigach area, with event listings and things to do.

Culag Community Woodland Trust
culagwoods.org.uk
The CCWT manage the Culag Woods and Little Assynt Estate. Their website has information about both, along with event listings.

Assynt Crofters' Trust
theassyntcrofters.co.uk
The Trust manages the North Assynt Estate, which was bought by the local crofters in a historic buy-out in 1993. Their site has information about the local community, history and local events.

Assynt Angling Information
assyntanglinginfo.org.uk
Assynt is a world-class angling destination, and this site has all the information to help you find the best spots and book a permit.

Discover Assynt
discoverassynt.co.uk
A list of facilities, attractions and things to do in the Assynt area.

Assynt Field Club
assyntwildlife.org.uk
A free organisation aimed at encouraging the study and enjoyment of Assynt's wildlife, landscape and geology. Their website has a list of upcoming events, recent wildlife sightings, and information about projects past and present.

Assynt Fire and Water
assyntfireandwater.aocarchaeology.com
A trove of information about local history and archaeology.

Contributing Photographers

Dougie Cunningham: leadinglines.net
facebook.com/leadinglines
instagram: @leading_lines

Chris Puddephatt: jacksonphotography.co.uk
facebook.com/jacksonphotographycouk
instagram: @chrispuddephatt

Dave McBain: davar-lochinver.co.uk
facebook.com/DavarLochinver

Justine Ritchie: justineritchie.com
facebook.com/JustineRitchiePhotographer
instagram: @justine.ritchie

Tim Hamlet: hamletmountaineering.com
facebook.com/hamletmountaineering
instagram: @ hamlet_mountaineering

Mairi-Anne MacLeod: tidalgifts.co.uk
facebook.com/tidalgifts
instagram: @mairiannemacleod

David Haines and **Phil Jones** also very kindly supplied photographs, but do not maintain an online presence. Many thanks to all contributors!

Notes